A Funny Thing Happened on the Way to the Podium

A Funny Thing
Happened on the Way
to the Podium

The Speaker's Complete Guide
to Great Jokes, Anecdotes, and Stories

Herbert V. Prochnow

Prima Publishing

35933

PRO

PRIMA PUBLISHING and colophon are registered trademarks of Prima Communications, Inc.

Previously published under the title *Speaker's & Toastmaster's Handbook* by Prima Publishing, 1993

Library of Congress Cataloging-in-Publication Data on file

LC Card number 98-26824
ISBN 0-7615-1452-X

98 99 00 01 02 03 AA 10 9 8 7 6 5 4 3 2 1
Printed in the United States of America

How to Order
Single copies may be ordered from Prima Publishing, P.O. Box 1260BK, Rocklin, CA 95677; telephone (916) 632-4400. Quantity discounts are also available. On your letterhead, include information concerning the intended use of the books and the number of books you wish to purchase.

Visit us online at www.primapublishing.com

CONTENTS

PREFACE

This book contains more than 500 humorous stories, 292 humorous definitions, 500 epigrams and quips, 100 stories from unusual lives and comments by unusual people, 190 statements on important subjects by great thinkers, 200 wise and witty proverbs, and 160 unusual quotations, both humorous and serious, from world leaders through the ages.

The 2,000 plus items in this book will add sparkle to speeches and introductions and enliven conversation. They provide humor, help emphasize a point in a speech or in conversation so it will not be forgotten, or add inspiration to a speech. The epigrams, literary quotations, anecdotes from biographies, humorous stories, inspiring illustrations, and interesting facts and ideas enhance general discussions and informal meetings and help present ideas colorfully and effectively.

General readers who enjoy wit tersely expressed will also find this a pleasant and enjoyable book to browse through on many occasions.

Herbert V. Prochnow

Chapter 1

HUMOROUS STORIES

Progress

Two men were examining the output of the new computer in their department. Eventually one of them remarked: "Do you realize it would take 400 men 250 years to make a mistake this big?"

Say It Now

Husband with hand on television knob: "Mae, do you have anything to say before the football season starts?"

Instructions Not Clear

The instructor in the mechanics class spoke to one of his students: "I'm putting this rivet in the correct position; when I nod my head, hit it real hard with your hammer." The student did, and the instructor woke up the next day in the hospital.

Right

The biology teacher said to her class, "And from the skunk we get fur. Isn't that right class?"

"Yes," said a voice in the back, "as fur as possible."

Modern History

The history professor had been intoning for the better part of an hour on British royal lineage. He droned on, "Mary followed Edward VI, didn't she?"

Class in unison: Yes, sir.

Professor: And who followed Mary?

Voice from the
rear of the room: Her little lamb.

Cuts Costs in the Future

Lady: This picture makes me look much older than I am.

Photographer: Well, that will certainly save you the expense of having one taken later on.

He Is Getting Along Well

"How are you getting along at home while your wife's away visiting her mother?"

"Fine. I've reached the height of efficiency. I can put on my socks from either end."

She Was Probably Right

Mother to small son at the table: "Twenty years from now you'll be telling some girl what a great cook I was; now be quiet and eat your dinner!"

Awkward Age

Father to neighbor: "My son happens to be at that awkward age. He doesn't know whether to give a girl his seat on the bus—or race her for it."

Attending to Business

Signs of the times—On a parked car in front of the city hall was the sign: Attorney inside attending to business. When the lawyer returned he found this notice on the car: Policeman outside attending to business.

Converted

A plane, blinded by clouds and snow, ran out of gas and crashed. Most of the crew bailed out to safety. Said one crew member: "I went up an atheist and came down a Methodist."

T-Bone with Meat

Sign in a restaurant window: T-Bone—25 cents. In fine print underneath the sign: With meat—$15.

Smart Question

"I'm six!" exclaimed a little boy to his neighbor on his birthday. "Six years old, imagine that," said the neighbor. "You're not even as tall as my umbrella!"

"How old is your umbrella?" was the response.

Good Endorsement

A young bride tried to cash her husband's paycheck at a bank. "You need an endorsement," the teller told her.

The bride thought for a moment and then wrote on the back of the check: "My husband is a wonderful man. Sally Johnson."

What He Thinks

Mrs. Smith: I just can't understand it. The people next door don't have a stereo. They don't have a color television. She never wears any nice jewelry, and they aren't even members of the country club. And to top it off, they drive one of those subcompact cars. What do you think?

Mr. Smith: I think it's great. They've got money.

That Explains It

After correcting the class papers, the teacher remarked to a particular student, "I just can't understand how one person can make so many mistakes on his work."

Her student thought for a bit and then commented, "It wasn't just one person. My dad helped with the assignment."

What College-Bred Means

A small boy asked his father what "college-bred" meant. "Son," his dad replied, "college-bred comes from the flour of youth and the dough of old age."

Common Experience

Mr. Smith: Your wife looks magnetic.

Mr. Jones: She should—everything she has on is charged.

Conservative Figure

A New Englander was listening to the Florida resident bragging about the weather.

"Do you mean to say," he asked, "that in Florida you have 365 days of sunshine every year?"

"That's right," replied the man from the Sunshine State. "And that's a mighty conservative estimate too."

A Little Different

Father: Tell me, Susie, how did your test go today?

Susie: Well, I did just what George Washington did.

Father: How's that?

Susie: I went down in history.

Six Will Do It

A man stopped by the florist's to buy some flowers for his girlfriend.

"You want to say it with flowers, sir?" the florist asked. "How about three dozen American Beauty roses?"

"Make it half a dozen," the fellow said. "I'm a man of few words."

What You Are

The teacher, who had asked her pupils to write essays on anatomy, was quite amused at one of the results.

One little girl wrote: "Your head is kind of hard and your brains are in it and your hair grows on it. Your face is in front of your head where you eat. Your neck is what keeps your head off your shoulders, which are sort of like shelves where you hook the straps to your bib overalls. Your arms are what you have to pitch a softball with and so you can reach for the muffins at breakfast. Your fingers stick out of your hands so you can scratch, throw a curve, and add arithmetic. Your legs are what you have so you can run to first base; your feet are what you run on, and your toes are what gets stubbed. And that's all there is of you, except what is inside. But I've never seen that."

Didn't Need Help

Waiter: May I help you with that soup, sir?

Diner: What do you mean? I don't need any help.

Waiter: Sorry, sir. From the sound I thought you might wish to be dragged ashore.

Smart Lad

The teacher was explaining to her pupils: "Quite a number of the plants and flowers have the prefix 'dog.' There's the dog-rose and the dog-violet, for instance. Can any of you name another?"

There was a silence, and then a happy look appeared on the face of a youngster in the back row.

"Teacher," he asked politely, "how about collie-flower?"

He Had an Advantage

Two small boys at the Salvation Army dinner put their grimy hands side by side on the tablecloth.

"Mine's dirtier'n yourn!" exclaimed one, triumphantly.

"Huh!" said the other; "you're two years older'n me! Wait'll mine git as old as yourn!"

She Didn't Know

The psychiatrist asked the exasperated mother: "Does your son have a behavior problem?"

"I don't know ... I've never seen him behaving," she replied.

Choosing a Career

An education survey polled college freshmen as to what careers they hoped to follow. Here are some of their choices: "Bsness, Buseness, Physist, Finnance, Holesail Salisman, Denestry, Technection, Airnotics, Treacher, Stewardes, Secteral, and Engenering." One wrote "Undesided," and another was "Undisided."

Can Figures Lie?

The instructor was trying to drive home some truths. "Figures can't lie," he declared. "For instance, if 1 man can build a house in 12 days, 12 men can build it in 1 day."

A puzzled student interrupted: "Then 288 men can build it in 1 hour, 17,280 in 1 minute, and 1,036,809 in 1 second."

While the instructor was still gasping, the ready reckoner went on: "And if 1 ship can cross the Atlantic in 6 days, 6 ships can cross it in 1 day. 'Figures can't lie,' can they?"

No Trouble

Once upon a time there were two morons. One of them called the other on the telephone at three o'clock in the morning. "Hello, is this University one one one one?"

After a while came the answer, "Nope, this is University eleven eleven."

"Well then, sorry to bother you at this time of night."

"Oh, that's all right; I had to get up to answer the telephone anyway."

Exam Answers

Here are some answers found on grade school exam papers:

"Climate lasts a long time, but the weather is only a few days."

"A planet is a body of earth surrounded by sky."

"The feminine of bachelor is lady-in-waiting."

"A sure-footed animal is an animal that when it kicks does not miss anything."

Couldn't Fool Him

The chemistry professor was demonstrating the properties of various acids. "Now, I am going to drop this silver coin into this glass of acid. Will it dissolve?"

A student in the rear promptly answered, "No sir."

"No?" queried the professor, a glint in his eye. "Perhaps the young man will explain to the class why the silver coin won't dissolve."

The young student rose and said, "Because if it would, you wouldn't have dropped it in."

A Warning

A political speaker, warning against higher taxes, said, "If you don't stop shearing the wool off the sheep that lays the golden egg, you'll pump it dry."

Learning Early

A little girl and her mother shopped in the department store all day. As they made their last purchase and prepared to leave, a hostess handed the child a lollipop. "What do you say?" prompted the mother.

"Charge it," the little one replied.

How It Happened

There once was a dachshund so long that he hadn't any notion of how long it took to notify his tail of an emotion. And so it happened, while his eyes were full of woe and sadness, his little tail went wagging on because of previous gladness.

Modern Farming

Visitor: So your son is planning to run the farm when he gets out of college?

Farmer: Well, at least he's beginning to take an interest in it. He's just been showing me where we could have a golf course and how easy it would be to turn the barn into a clubhouse.

The Village Smithy

Beneath the spreading chestnut tree the village smithy snoozes; no nag, since 1923, has been to him for shoeses.

Don't Worry

A baby sardine was happily swimming in the ocean near its mother when it saw its first submarine. The mother quickly reassured her frightened offspring. "Don't worry dear. It's just a can of people."

Diplomacy

Franz Liszt, no less a diplomat than a musician, had a stock reply for young women who demanded unmerited praise of their singing.

"Maestro," a young woman would inquire, "do you think I have a good voice?"

"Ah, my dear young lady," Liszt would reply with the utmost sincerity, " 'good' is not the word to describe it!"

Helpful

"No, you can't interest me in a vacuum cleaner. Try the lady next door—I always use hers and it's just terrible."

She Remembered

The groom found his pretty bride weeping when he came home from the office. "I feel terrible," she told him. "When I was pressing your suit, I burned a hole right in the seat of your trousers."

"Forget it, honey," he said. "You must have forgotten that I have an extra pair of pants for that suit."

"Oh, I remembered," answered the bride. "I cut a piece from them to patch the hole."

Needs Help

The first graders were attending their first music lesson. The teacher was trying to begin at the beginning. She drew a musical staff on the blackboard and asked a little girl to come up and write a note on it.

The little girl went to the blackboard, looked thoughtful for a moment, and then wrote, "Dear Aunt Mary, I am well and hope you are the same. Susan."

Do You Know?

How much did Philadelphia Pa? How much does Columbus O? How many eggs did New Orleans La? What grass did Joplin Mo? We call Minneapolis Minn; why not Annapolis Ann? If you can't tell us why, we'll bet Topeka Kan.

Be Careful

A sign in the window of a beauty parlor reads: "Don't whistle at a girl leaving here. It may be your grandmother."

Good Reason

A boy walked up to the box office at a movie theater one Wednesday afternoon at one o'clock and handed the cashier the money for a ticket.

"It's only one o'clock," she said to him. "Why aren't you in school?"

"Oh, it's all right," he said, "I've got the measles."

Thoughtful Opinion

Two goats wandered into an alley behind a movie house, looking for their dinner. They found a can of film, which one of the goats devoured, along with the can.

"How was it?" his companion asked.

"I think the book was better," he replied.

Psychiatrist

Two publishers ran into each other at the door of the psychiatrist's office.

"Hello," said one, "you coming or going?"

"If I knew that," replied the other, "I wouldn't be here."

Of Course

"How did I get here?" the baby ear of corn asked its mother.

"The stalk brought you."

Saving Time

Every busy man should have a wife, so he won't need to waste so much time making up his mind about things.

Thoughtful

Teacher to a class of small children: "Will all those who think they are stupid stand up."

For a moment no one got up, then one little boy stood. "Billy," said the teacher, "do you think you are stupid?"

"No, teacher," was the answer, "I just didn't like to see you standing up by yourself!"

They Don't Live There

"I like the scenery around here," commented a tourist to a local New Englander, "but most of the people are so strange."

"That's true," replied the New Englander, "but most of them go home at the end of the summer."

Very Smart

"Looks like you have a smart dog there," remarked a friend.

"Smart? All I have to tell him is 'Are you coming or aren't you?' And he either comes or he doesn't."

He Believed

Teacher: Stevie, do you believe that George Washington could have pitched a dollar across the Potomac River as the saying goes?

Stevie: I guess so. Our history book says he pitched his camp across the Delaware River when the British were pursuing him.

Poland

A Polish worker walks into a bank to deposit his paycheck.

But he has heard about Poland's economic problems, and he asks what would happen to his money if the bank collapsed.

"All our deposits are guaranteed by the finance ministry, sir," the teller replies.

"But what if the finance ministry goes broke?" the worker asks.

"Then the government will intercede to protect the working class," the teller says.

"But what if the government goes broke?" the worker asks.

"Our socialist comrades in the Soviet Union naturally will come to our assistance," the teller responds with growing irritation.

"And if the Soviet Union goes broke?" the worker asks.

"Idiot!" the teller snorts. "Isn't that worth losing one lousy paycheck?"

There Is a Difference

Mr. Green: My wife is very poetic; she gets up at sunrise and says, "Lo, the morn!"

Mr. Gray: What! You lucky man. My wife gets up and says, "Mow the lawn!"

Practical Idea

Why doesn't somebody cross electric blankets with toasters so that people could pop out of bed early each morning?

It Always Does

Professor: What happens when the human body is immersed in water?

Student: The telephone rings.

Next Question

Teacher: Tommy, name five things that contain milk.

Tommy: Butter, cheese, ice cream, and two cows.

Not Always

It was a wise youngster who, on being asked, "What is the chief end of man?" replied, "The end that's got the head on."

Wanted to Be Ready

Bobby: Mom, when we have company for dinner today, do I have to eat my pie with a fork?

Mom: Yes, indeed you do.

Bobby: Well, have you got enough pie so I could practice with a fork for a while before the company comes?

Of Course Not

"Yes, I used to shoot tigers in Alaska," asserted the big game hunter, boastfully.

"But there are no tigers in Alaska," protested a listener.

"Certainly not!" exclaimed the hunter. "I got them all!"

He Did

Head cook: Didn't I tell you to notice when the soup boiled over?

Assistant: I did—it was at half-past ten.

One Answer

Teacher: Students, who is man's noblest friend?

Timmy: The hot dog—it feeds the hand that bites it.

Hard Worker

Boss: How is it that you're only carrying one sack when the other hands are carrying two?

Worker: Well, maybe they're just too lazy to make two trips like I do.

Doesn't Need a Den

Two youngsters were discussing their fathers one afternoon, especially the little peculiarities in their behavior. One small boy asked the other, "Does your daddy have a den?"

"Nope," replied his little friend, "he just growls all over the place at our house."

A Five Star Restaurant

A motorist and his wife stopped at an unimpressive restaurant. Both ordered iced tea with their meal, the wife adding, "And be sure my glass is absolutely clean!" A second waiter appeared a few minutes later with the tea. "Here they are," he said. "Which one gets the clean glass?"

Great Shot

A group of freshmen taking astronomy had their first class in the observation laboratory one evening. The professor went to the telescope and began to make an observation. Just then a star fell.

"That was a fine shot," one of the students said. "Why, he hardly had time to take aim."

Different Meaning

"Mother, what does 'apt' mean?" little Billy asked one day after returning from school.

"Why, dear, it means 'smart, quick to learn.' Why do you ask?"

"Oh, nothing much," said Billy airily. "The teacher just told me today I was apt to flunk."

Be Careful

Little Johnny was in one of his very bad and disobedient moods. In answer to his mother's remonstrations that he behave himself, he said: "Give me a nickel and I'll be good."

"Give you a nickel!" She scolded: "Why Johnny, you shouldn't be good for a nickel, you should be good for nothing—like your father."

Getting Rich

A country superstar is someone who gets rich by singing about how wonderful it is to be poor.

—*The Monroe County Democrat*

He Needs Help

Patient: Doctor, I can't remember anything from one minute to the next. I'm worried.

Psychiatrist: Now just how long has this been going on?

Patient: How long has what been going on?

Hard Question

Little Bobby took a long look at the old man and asked, "Were you on the ark, Grandpa, when the flood came?"

"No, certainly not," replied his grandfather.

"Well, then why weren't you drowned?"

Too Often Neglected

When a small boy saw a Bible, not too recently dusted, lying on a shelf in his home, he asked his mother whose book it was. "It is God's book," she said. "Well," the boy commented, "don't you think we should return it? Nobody seems to read it here!" —*Christian Advocate*

The Ten Commandments

A young woman was mailing the old family Bible to her brother in a distant city. The postal clerk examined the package carefully and inquired whether it contained anything breakable.

"Nothing but the Ten Commandments," was her quick reply.

Time Flies

Frustrated diner: "You tell me you're the same fellow who took my order. Somehow, I expected a much older waiter."

A New Channel

The geography teacher asked Billy to describe the English Channel.

"I don't know the answer. We don't get that channel on our TV set," was his reply.

Real Progress

The state detectives sent out six different pictures of a suspected bank robber. A deputy in a small town several miles away sent the following letter a few days later: "Have captured five of them and am on the trail of the sixth."

His Viewpoint

The proud parents took their little boy to church for the first time. When the members of the choir entered in their flowing, white robes, the child whispered: "Look, they're all going to get their hair cut."

It Makes You Lose Weight

The secretary ran into a friend at the lunch counter and saw that the friend was eating a plate of cottage cheese.

"Are you trying to lose weight?" the secretary asked.

"Oh, no," the friend replied. "I'm on a low salary diet."

Just Remember

"If life may seem to trick you, and give you the boot, just remember that there's only one thing can lick you, and that's the guy inside your suit."

What He Pays For

The baldheaded gentleman asked his barber, "Why charge me the full price for cutting my hair—there's so little of it?"

"Well," said the barber, "actually I make little charge for cutting it. What you're really paying for is my searching for it!"

Smart Hens

The young married woman and her husband had moved to the country to live, and she was on her first visit back to the city.

"So, you like country life," her father said. "Are your hens good layers?"

"They're experts," the young lady replied. "They haven't laid a bad egg yet."

Her Training Will Help

A girl was away at college. Her father was asked, "What is your daughter going to do after she graduates?"

The father replied, "From the training she's getting, I know she'll become a great professional fund raiser."

Good Question

Dismayed by the size of the St. Bernard dog given him for his birthday, the little boy asked, "Is he for me, or am I for him?"

His Wife Has a Problem Also

"Well, John, how does it feel to be a grandfather?"

"Oh, it's good news, of course, but I'll have to get used to the idea of being married to a grandmother!"

That's Different

"Happiness," claimed the philosopher, "is the pursuit of something, not the catching of it."

"Have you ever," interrupted a listener, "chased the last bus on a rainy night?"

Why Hold Back?

Lady: I'll give a quarter, not because you deserve it, but because it pleases me to do so.

Hobo: Thank you, ma'am, but why not make it a dollar and really enjoy yourself?

Hard Decision

Barber: You want your hair parted exactly in the middle, sir?

Customer: That's what I said, didn't I?

Barber: Then I'll have to pull one out, sir. You have five hairs.

Good Question

A class of second graders was visiting an Egyptian museum with their teacher. "Why," one little boy wanted to know, "are there so many mummies and no daddies?"

Anything to Help

The diner was agitated because the waiter had brought him a knife and a fork but no spoon.

"This coffee," he said pointedly, "is going to be pretty hot to stir with my fingers."

The waiter reddened and beat a hasty retreat to the kitchen. He returned shortly with another cup of coffee.

"This one isn't so hot, sir," he beamed.

Ready to Go

Coach Smith was dejected because his football team was losing by a large margin. He looked down the bench at his substitutes and yelled: "Okay, Jones, go in there and get ferocious!"

Jones, who hadn't been on the field all season, jumped up with a start and said, "Sure coach. What's his number?"

One More Would Be Enough

"Another bite like that, young lady," a mother told her young daughter, "and you'll have to leave this table."

"Another bite like that and I'll be finished," was the little one's reply.

In Doubt

Customer: Remember that cheese you sold me yesterday?

Grocer: Yes, madam.

Customer: Did you say it was imported or deported from Switzerland?

It's Easy

The golfer stepped up to the tee and drove off. The ball sailed down the fairway, leaped onto the green, and rolled into the hole. The golfer threw his club into the air with excitement.

"Have you suddenly gone crazy?" asked his wife, who was trying to learn the game.

"Why, I just did a hole in one!" yelled the golfer, a gleam of delight in his eyes.

"Did you?" his wife asked placidly. "Do it again dear, I didn't see you."

He Was Certain

Father was sitting in the armchair one evening when his little son came in and showed him a new penknife, which he said he had found in the street.

"Are you sure it was lost?" the father inquired.

"Of course it was lost! I saw the man looking for it!" replied the youngster.

Only the Top

Two sailors, at sea for the first time, were looking out over the mighty ocean. Said one, "That's the most water I ever saw."

The other replied, "You ain't seen nothin' yet. That's just the top of it."

Slow to Learn

The junior sales manager complained of aches and pains to his wife. Neither could account for his trouble. Arriving home one night from work, he informed her, "I finally discovered why I've been feeling so miserable. We got some ultramodern office furniture two weeks ago, and I just learned today that I've been sitting in the wastebasket."

Good Reason

"There are a lot of twins being born these days," said Smith, looking up from his newspaper.

"Naturally," said his companion and added, "The shape the world is in nowadays, the poor kids are afraid to come into it alone."

Ready to Blast Off

After a long dreary Saturday during which our two sons had been particularly rambunctious, my wife had reached the end of her patience. "Get ready for bed!" she commanded.

The boys headed for their room, and I overheard Tom— eight years old—say, "We'd better get a move on. She's on the countdown and ready to blast off."

Taking No Chances

The professor returned to class with the exam papers and requested that all the students sit down. "If you stood up, it is conceivable that you might form a circle—in which case I might be arrested for maintaining a dope ring."

Good Advice

A speaker at a luncheon gave a tremendous talk and received a standing ovation. The president of the club was so impressed that he said to the speaker, "Everyone here is enthused. Won't you please say a few words since we have ten minutes left of our regular time?"

The speaker said, "Once there was a little baby cabbage who sad to his mother, 'Mommy, I'm worried about something. As I sit in this row of cabbages and grow and grow day after day, how will I know when to stop growing?' 'The rule to follow,' said the mamma cabbage, 'is to quit when you are a head.' "

Stop Acting

The professor seemed greatly irritated at the action of a student. "Listen here young man," he exclaimed, "are you the professor of this class?"

"No, sir, I'm not," answered the young man boldly.

"Well, then, stop acting like a fool!"

A Young Salesman

A youngster walked into a bank the other day to open an account for $25. The bank's cashier gave him a benign smile and asked how he had accumulated so much money.

"Selling Christmas cards," said the lad.

"Well, you've done very well. Sold them to lots of people, obviously."

"Nope," said the little boy proudly, "I sold all of them to one family—their dog bit me."

That's Different

Two laborers were hired to paint some flagpoles. One fellow stood on the other's shoulder and reached up as far as he could. The superintendent passed by and wanted to know what they were doing. "We've got to measure how high the pole is so we can know how much paint we'll need."

The super said, "Nonsense. Take the flagpole down and lay it on the ground. Then you can measure it."

One of the laborers said, "A lot you know. We want to find out how high it is, not how long it is."

In the Old Days

Bothered by the frequent coffee breaks and other interruptions in the modern workday, the veteran plumber said, "Back in the days when I was taught my trade, we never did any of this goldbricking. After we'd install two lengths of pipe, our foreman would turn on the water and if we couldn't keep ahead of it, we'd get fired."

Real Problem

A physician recommended to one of his patients that he lose about 40 pounds. The doctor's instructions were to run 5 miles a day for the next 100 days. The overweight patient called the doctor exactly 100 days later and complained that he was unhappy with the weight-loss program.

"But haven't you lost the weight?" questioned the physician.

"Sure I did," the patient replied. "But I'm 500 miles from home!"

Correct Answer

Teacher: Name three collective nouns.

Pupil: Dustpan, wastebasket, and vacuum cleaner.

Say That Again

Customer at
soda fountain: I want a plain soda water without flavor.

Clerk: What flavor do you want it without?

Customer: What flavors have you got?

Clerk: We have chocolate, pineapple, vanilla, and caramel.

Customer: Well, I wanted it without strawberry.

Clerk: I'm sorry, but we're all out of strawberry. Would you just as soon have it without chocolate?

Cheaper

Some old-timers were discussing a mutual friend. Said one, "Poor old John seems to be living in the past."

"Well, why not?" replied the other man. "It's a lot cheaper."

He Couldn't Sleep

A man put up at a hotel, and the clerk warned that the man in the next room was very nervous. When the man went to his room, he thoughtlessly threw his shoe down very hard. Then he happened to think of the poor nervous guy, so he laid the other shoe down very gently. He went to bed, and about two hours later he heard a rap at the door. He asked who it was, and the nervous man said: "For heaven's sake, throw that other shoe down, will you?"

Looking Ahead

Little Carol met the minister as she came out of a drugstore with an ice cream cone.

"Why didn't you give your money to the missions?" asked the minister.

"Oh," she replied, "I buy ice cream cones and the druggist gives the money to the missions."

It Was Worse Then

The kindly old lady was much impressed with the street beggar. "Oh, you poor man!" she exclaimed. "It must be dreadful to be lame. But you know, it could be worse. I think it would be much worse if you were blind!"

"You're tellin' me lady," responded the beggar. "When I was blind, people was all the time givin' me pennies."

No Time

Little Alice came into the house all bedraggled and weeping.

"My goodness," cried her mother, "what a sight you are! How on earth did it happen?"

"I'm s-so s-sorry, Mommy, but I fell into a puddle of mud."

"What! With your new dress on?"

"Y-y-yes, I didn't have time to change it."

He Certainly Is

"Billy sure is conceited, isn't he?"

"I'll say. Did you know that on his last birthday he sent a note of congratulations to his parents?"

His Technique

A stout gentleman was discussing his tennis technique.

"My brain barks out a command to my body: 'Run forward speedily. Start right away. Slam the ball gracefully over the net.'"

"And then what happens?" his friend inquired.

"And then," the out-of-shape fellow replied, "my body stops and says: 'Who, me?'"

It Helps

Young husband to his neighbor: "My wife is a good cook. She can prepare the best meal you ever thaw!"

Smart Customer Relations

A kindergartner made a new friend on the big school bus that picked him up and took him home each day. The new-found friend turned out to be a new bus driver, an important person in the life of a five-year-old—his link between home and school.

"I really like her," the child announced to his parents, "because she treats me like I'm a people!"

Sell Him

A farm magazine received this letter from a reader: "I have a horse that sometimes appears to be normal, and at other times is very lame. Can you tell me what I should do?"

The publisher sent this reply: "The next time your horse appears normal, sell him."

Good Reason

Foreman: Why are you late?

Worker: I had car trouble.

Foreman: What's wrong with your car?

Worker: I was late getting into it.

He Knows Them All

The parents were listening to their eight-year-old practicing away on his trumpet while their dog loudly howled at his side.

Finally, the father said: "Son, why don't you play something the dog doesn't know?"

Meets the Test

Teacher: Bobby, if you don't settle down and become more serious, you'll never grow up to be a very responsible man.

Bobby: Why, I'm a responsible boy even now. Every time something happens at home, Mom always tells me I'm responsible.

Wrong Question

Politician: Well, dear, I've been reelected!

Wife: Honestly?

Politician: I don't see that there's any need for you to bring that up.

Real Talent

"My grandfather plays the piano by ear," said the boy.

"Well, if we must boast—my grandfather fiddles with his beard," was the other child's ready reply.

Think Twice

Before criticizing your wife's faults, remember that it may have been those very defects that prevented her from catching a better husband.

No Rest

"As maintenance of this churchyard is becoming increasingly difficult and expensive, it will be appreciated if parishioners will cut the grass around their own graves."

—*Notice in a local newspaper in Essex, England*

Advice

"I saw a psychiatrist today about my memory lapses."

"Oh really?" What did he say?"

"He said I'd have to pay my bill in advance."

He Knew It

A second-grade student was talking to a friend about the recent fire in their school. "I knew it was going to happen, we'd been practicing for it all year."

She Asked First

A lady with her checkbook in a muddle phoned her bank for help.

"What balance do you show?" asked the bank clerk.

"I asked you first," replied the caller.

Very Lucky

When Diogenes was looking for an honest man, a friend asked what luck he was having.

Diogenes replied: "Oh, pretty fair; I still have my lantern."

It Helps

A recent bride bragged to another newlywed, "I have my husband eating out of my hand."

Replied her friend: "Saves time on dishwashing, doesn't it?"

Smart Lady

"When my wife wants money, she calls me handsome."

"Handsome?"

"Yeah, hand some over."

Grocer's Mistake

"I baked a sponge cake for you darling," the young bride announced, "but it didn't turn out quite right. I think the grocer gave me the wrong kind of sponges."

A Big Job

"I'm sorry I'm late, Mom," said ten-year-old Jimmy as he rushed home from school. "We were making a science display, and I had to stay to finish the universe."

Not an Authority

A comedian says the people do not appreciate new jokes. How does he know?

Never

Skeptical customer:	Can this coat be worn out in the rain without hurting it?
Fur salesman:	Did you ever see a skunk carrying an umbrella?

He Sneezed a Sneeze

I sneezed a sneeze into the air; it fell to earth I knew not where. But hard and cold were the looks of those in whose vicinity I snoze.

Quick to Learn

A poodle and a cocker spaniel met in the park. The poodle said, "My name's Fifi, what's yours?"

Replied the spaniel, "I think it's Down Boy."

Speaks from Experience

The youngster told his little brother he could be spared much toil by refusing to spell his first word. "The minute you spell 'cat,' you're trapped," he said. "After that the words get harder and harder."

They Can't Help It

A scientist says a great many animals laugh. How can they help it when they watch what people do?

He Gets Respect

The proprietor of a grocery store had shown marked attention to one of his customers. Another customer, a newcomer to the town, had witnessed the proceedings and remarked, "I noticed you treated your last customer with some deference."

"Yes," replied the proprietor, "he's one of our early settlers."

"But he doesn't appear over forty to me," said the customer.

"I don't know how old he is," answered the grocer. "But I do know he always settles his bill on the first of the month."

Tried to Help

Two Cub Scouts, whose younger brother had fallen into the lake, rushed home to mother with tears in their eyes.

"We try to give him artificial respiration," one of them sobbed, "but he keeps getting up and walking away."

Not Too Fussy

Employer: I'm sorry I can't hire you, but I just couldn't find enough work to keep you busy.

Applicant: You'd be surprised at how little it takes.

Almost Perfect

"How're you getting along with your new second-hand car?" Mr. Smith asked.

"Well," said Mr. Jones, "there's only one part of it that doesn't make a noise, and that's the horn."

Covering Up

Architects cover their mistakes with ivy. Lawyers visit theirs in jail. Advertising executives put theirs on television, and cooks cover theirs with mayonnaise.

Progress

"I received a letter from my grandson in the Army," Mrs. Jones told her neighbor.

"How's he doing?"

"Just fine. Says he recently made court martial."

Not Going That Way

A Mississippi River steamboat was stopped in the mouth of a tributary stream, owing to the dense fog. An inquisitive passenger asked the captain what the cause of delay was.

"Can't see up the river," was the captain's laconic reply.

"But I can see the stars overhead," the passenger said to him.

"Yes," came back the captain, "but unless the boilers bust, we ain't goin' that way."

Very Careful

A museum curator said to the moving man: "Be very careful when you carry this vase, it's 2,000 years old."

"You can count on me," the moving man said. "I'll carry it just as if it were new."

Not Necessary

One business partner to the other, on a fishing trip: "We forgot to lock the safe!"

"What's the difference? We're both here, aren't we?"

Please Note

A notice in the *Gazette* of the Red Lake Falls, Minnesota, some time ago read: "St. Joseph's and Oak Grove Cemeteries will be closed November 15 for the winter. Residents of the area should govern themselves accordingly."   —*Sunshine Magazine*

Think Before You Speak

At a dinner party, a shy young fellow kept trying to think of something nice to say to the hostess. At last he saw his chance when the hostess turned to him and said, "What a small appetite you have, Mr. Brown."

"Sitting next to you," he remarked gallantly, "would cause anyone to lose his appetite."

Salesmanship

Salesmen sometimes need considerable linguistic talent as well as sales ability to make contact with their customers. A salesman calling on prospects in a Pennsylvania Dutch district rang and rang at one doorbell, but nobody answered. As he was walking away, he noticed a neat sign hanging from the knob: "Doorbell don't make; bump!"

Go Ahead

An airline ticket agent was being given a particularly rough time by a woman who complained about a delay in the departure time. She said, "Young man, I could stick a feather in my ear and get there faster."

"Madam," replied the agent calmly, "the runways are clear."

Take Your Choice

The cowboy had a new horse that was very stubborn and kicked so violently that one day one of its hooves got caught in the stirrup. The man said angrily to the horse, "There's no room on the saddle for both of us; if you're going to get on, I'm going to get off."

Meant Well

People do not always mean what they say. A kind-hearted woman raised money to send to an area where there had been a disaster. It took her longer to get the money together than she had anticipated, and she feared it would be late in arriving. So she sent this note with the contribution: "We hope the suffering is not all over."

Followed Instructions

Boss: Didn't you get the letter I sent you?

Office boy: Yes, sir. I read it on the inside and on the outside. On the inside it said, "You're fired!" On the outside it read, "Return in five days." So—here I am!

So It Seemed

Little boy: Daddy! Look, I pulled this cornstalk up all by myself.

Daddy: What a strong boy!

Little boy: Sure. The whole world had hold of the other end.

No Mozart

Neighbor: Where's your little sister, Mindy?

Mindy: In the house playing a duet ... I finished first.

A Little Late

A second-floor tenant called to the resident below and shouted: "If you don't stop playing those drums, I'll go crazy."

"I guess it's too late," came the reply. "I stopped playing them an hour ago."

Do You Think?

At night, before I sleep, I lie
And think and think, and wonder why.

Why tables have legs, and cannot walk;
Why pitchers have mouths, and cannot talk;
Why needles have eyes, and cannot wink;
Why pins have heads, and cannot think;
Why houses have wings, and cannot fly;
Why flowers have beds, and cannot lie;
Why clocks have hands, and cannot write;
Why combs have teeth, and cannot bite.

I think and think till I cannot sleep,
And have to start in counting sheep!

It Changed Him

A movie executive, famous for his long after-dinner speeches, now expresses himself with brevity. Asked to explain his reformation, he replied: "It was a remark I overheard. During a pause in one of my speeches, one man said to another, 'What follows this speaker?' The other man said, 'Wednesday.' "

Bad News and Good News

One banker has a new sign in his office: "There's good news and bad news."
"The bad news is that we can't predict interest rates."
"The good news is that we finally realize it."

Be Fair and Help

The burglars tied and gagged the cashier after extracting the combination to the safe and herded the other employees into a separate room under guard. After they rifled the safe and were about to leave, the cashier made desperate pleading noises through the gag. Moved by curiosity, one of the burglars loosened the gag.
"Please," whispered the cashier, "take the books too. I'm $6,500 short."

She Loves Gardening

The man with the kink in his back said to his sympathetic neighbor: "My wife loves gardening. I don't think there's anything she'd rather see me do."

Hold It

"Now in case anything should go wrong with this experiment," said the professor of chemistry, "we and the laboratory will be blown sky-high. Now come a little closer, so you can follow me."

Changing Times

"An old-timer is one who used to drop the boy off at school on his way to work. Now he has a boy who drops him off at work on his way to school."

He Likes It

Waitress: This is your fifth cup, sir. You must really like the coffee.

Diner: I sure do. That's why I'm willing to drink all this water to get a little of it.

How Else?

An office manager was asking a female applicant if she had any unusual talents. She said she had won several prizes in crossword puzzle and slogan-writing contests.

"Sounds good," the manager told her, "but we want somebody who will be smart during office hours."

"Oh," said the applicant, "that was during office hours."

My Kingdom for a Horse

The critic said to the sculptor, "It's a fine statue, all right, but isn't that a rather odd position for a general to assume?"

"Maybe so," said the sculptor, "but I was halfway finished when the committee ran out of money and decided that they couldn't afford a horse for him."

He Remembered

The will of a wealthy man was being read, and the relatives all listened expectantly, especially his playboy nephew. Finally, the lawyer read: "And to my nephew, John, whom I promised not to forget in my will—'Hi there, John.' "

An Idea

Turkey addressing barnyard flock: "Here's the plan. We go on a hunger strike so that by Thanksgiving we're nothing but skin and bones."

Yes!

Are you in favor of progress, just so long as nobody changes anything?

He Believes in Signs

The other day a pupil sauntered in long after school was under way. "Bobbie," the teacher asked, "what made you so late?"

The little fellow stood a moment and then answered: "It's that warning sign, away down the street, you know, that says in great big letters: 'School ahead; go slow!' "

Now We Understand

"This is the fourth morning you've been late, Susan."

"Yes, ma'am," replied Susan, "I overslept."

"Where is the clock I gave you?"

"In my room, ma'am."

"Don't you wind it up?"

"Oh, yes! I wind it up, ma'am."

"And do you set the alarm?"

"Every night."

"But don't you hear the alarm in the morning, Susan?"

"No, ma'am. That's the trouble. You see, the thing goes off while I'm asleep."

Easier Then

It was the minute of rest between the ninth and tenth rounds, and the battered fighter sat on his stool, his seconds working furiously over his bleeding face.

"I think he's got you whipped," said his manager in disgust.

"Yeah," agreed the pugilist, gazing dizzily through nearly closed eyes. "I should have got him in the first round when he was by himself."

Understand?

The mother of one teenager caught on fast to jive talk. Her daughter asked, "Mom, may I hit the flick?"

"I'm afraid I don't read you," replied the mother.

"Oh, Mother," said the youngster, "you mean you don't know?" 'Hit the flick' is teen talk for 'go to the movies.' "

"In that case, ask me again after you rub the tub, scour the shower, spread the bed, and swish the dish."

Changing Jobs

A woman ready to go to the store stood at the door with her arms full of coats. Four little children stood at her side. Her husband, coming down the stairs, asked why she was standing there.

Handing him the coats, she said, "This time you put on the children's coats, and I'll honk the horn."

Remarkable

Slow waiter: This coffee is imported from Brazil.

Tired customer: Well, what do you know? It's still warm!

Looking Ahead

Weary father of a five-year-old to wife: "Talk! Talk! Thank goodness in a few years he'll be a teenager and we won't be able to communicate with him."

Obedience

"That was greedy of you, Tommy, to eat your little sister's share of pie."

"You told me, Mother, I was always to take her part," replied Tommy.

What He Observed

"Son, there is a wonderful example in the life of an ant," the father pointed out to his youngster. "Every day the ant goes to work and works all day. Every day the ant is busy, and in the end what happens?"

Unimpressed, the lad replied, "Someone steps on him."

Have Faith

A preacher who was in the habit of writing his sermons out carefully found himself at church one Sunday morning without his manuscript.

"As I have forgotten my notes," he said at the beginning of his sermon, "I will have to rely on the Lord for guidance. Next week I shall come better prepared."

Not Clear

The high school home economics teacher was explaining a recipe to her class and said, "When the mixture comes to a boil, add one tablespoon of milk."

One of her students then asked, "Is that level, or heaping?"

Not Selfish

Proud dad: Yes, son, I am a self-made man.

Junior: That's what I like about you, Dad. You take the blame for everything.

Fast Thinking

"The broadcast was great, Al! Marvelous! You're a pippin, Al!" the friend gushed.

"But heavens, man," shouted Jolson, "I haven't started yet!"

For a moment there was silence, then this comeback: "Yeah, but you forgot the three hours' difference in time. You're all through here."

Come Early

Notice in a church bulletin: Come to the morning service early if you want a good back seat!

Worth Trying

Moe: This liniment makes my arm smart!

Joe: Why don't you rub some on your head then?

Opinion

The woman: Aren't those chimes melodiously beautiful? Such harmony! So enchanting!

The man: You'll have to speak louder. Those confounded bells are making such a racket I can't hear you!

A Real Pane

A substitute speaker once tried to explain what a substitute was. He said, "You know, when a window pane is broken you stuff an old rag in it, and that is a substitute." He delivered his message, and at the close of the meeting a lady rushed up to him and said, "O Doctor, you are not an old rag. You're a real pane."

—Carl S. Winters

Modern

Parent: Isn't this toy rather complex for a small child?

Salesclerk: Oh, but this is an educational toy designed to provide the child with a means of adjusting to today's world. No matter what way the child assembles this toy— it's wrong.

Eggs-actly

The following was spotted in a grocery store window in Albany, New York: Strictly fresh eggs, 75 cents; fresh eggs, 60 cents; eggs, 50 cents.

Naturally

Why was King Arthur's time called the Dark Ages? Because there were so many knights.

Amazed

Reporter
interviewing
centenarian: How do you feel when you get up in the morning?

Centenarian: Amazed.

Logical

An accident victim was in the hospital recovering from a broken leg. "How are you being treated?" asked his concerned visitor.

"Well," replied the patient, "I can't kick."

Keeping One's Sense of Humor

A little girl had been sent away from the big table before the meal even began, and she sat there at her little table, miffed and pouting. After her father said grace, in the silence that ensued she was heard to say her prayer, which went like this: "I thank Thee, Lord, that Thou hast prepared a table before me in the presence of mine enemies." Which only goes to prove, incidentally, that even in the sacramental aspects of life one can keep one's sense of humor.

Of Course Not

Mother pigeon and her young son were preparing to migrate south, but the baby was afraid he wouldn't be able to fly that far.

"Don't worry," Mother pigeon said. "I'll tie one end of a piece of string around my leg and the other end to your neck. If you get tired, I can help you along."

Junior pigeon began to cry, "But I don't want to be pigeon-towed."

That's Different

The company's employment office was checking on an applicant's list of references.

"How long did this person work for you?" a former employer was asked.

"About six hours," was the brief reply.

"He informed us he'd been working for you a long time."

"Oh, yes," the ex-employer answered tersely, "he's been here for four years."

If You Ain't Sure

The third-grade teacher was trying to teach her class good grammar.

"You should never say 'I seen him do it,' " she told the class.

"Yeah," piped a voice from the back of the room. "Especially if you ain't sure he done it."

History

The guide on a sightseeing bus at Gettysburg kept telling the story of the famous Civil War battle in such a way that it sounded as if the South had had a great victory there. "Here is where two brave boys from Georgia captured an entire regiment of Northerners...."

A woman from Ohio spoke up: "Didn't the North win a single victory here?"

"Nope," was the answer. "And they aren't going to as long as I'm driving this bus!"

Out of Customary

Waitress: Will you have a piece of pie sir?

Man: Is it customary?

Waitress: No, it's cherry.

It Was Worth It

A fisherman was dragged into court for catching ten more trout than the law allowed. "Guilty or not guilty?" asked the judge.

"Guilty," said the sportsman.

"$25 and costs," remarked the judge.

After cheerfully paying the fine, the fisherman made one request: "And now, your honor, I'd respectfully like to ask for several copies of the court record to show my friends."

The Worst Part

Two little girls were discussing the subject of piggy banks.

"I think it's childish to save money that way," Mary said.

"I do too," Annie replied. "And I also believe that it encourages children to become misers."

"And that's not the worst of it," Mary exclaimed. "It turns parents into bank robbers!"

Is That Clear?

The portly sales manager was getting ready to leave his doctor's office after a routine examination.

"Here," said the doctor, "follow this diet, and I want to see three-fourths of you back here for a checkup in three months."

Isn't That Right?

A motorist was being examined for a driver's license.

Examiner: And what is the white line in the middle of the road for?

Motorist: Bicycles.

Seems Logical

"Hey, Larry, who's the father of all corn?"
    "I give up."
    "Popcorn, of course!"

Good Question

Stenographer: "Is 'waterworks' all one word, or do you spell it with a hydrant in the middle?"

He Had a Hard Time

A man walked into a doctor's waiting room. When the receptionist asked him what he had, he said, "Shingles."

She took his name, address, and medical insurance information and asked him to have a seat.

A nurse's aide called him into the office and asked what he had. Once again he said, "Shingles."

She took his weight, height, and complete medical history and led him to the examining room.

She then took a blood test and an electrocardiogram, checked his blood pressure, and told him to take off his clothes.

The doctor came in, looked at him, and asked what he had. He said, "Shingles."

"Where?" asked the obviously puzzled doctor.

"Outside in the truck," replied the man. "Where do you want them?"

Not Easy

Struggling with the English language, the foreigner was completely frustrated by the reasoning behind the pronunciation of words like tough, bough, though. He gave up when he read this newspaper headline: "Bazaar Pronounced Success."

He Knew

The lion tamer walked into a cage of lions at the circus, and everyone in the audience was nervous except one gray-haired man.

"I know what it feels like," he explained. "I drive a school bus myself."

A Big Star

A teenage girl was talking to a friend about a new pop singer she'd heard. "I know he's going to be a big star," she said confidently. "My father can't stand him."

What He Would Do

The teacher asked her students to write an essay, explaining what they would do if they each had $1 million. Every pupil except Teddy began writing. He sat in his chair twiddling his thumbs.

At the end of the class the teacher collected the papers. Teddy turned in a blank sheet.

"What is the meaning of this?" the teacher asked. "All the others have written two pages or more, but you've done nothing!"

"Well," replied Teddy, "if I had that much money, that's exactly what I'd do—nothing."

Or, the Ghost of Inflation Present

Gift counselor: "Something nice for your wife for about $20? Wait, I'll put you in touch with the Ghost of Christmas Past."

Very Quiet

Man to friend: "We're going to have a quiet Christmas this year—I'm giving the wife everything she's been hinting for."

Expensive Courtship

A woman had just broken her engagement to a doctor. Her

friend asked, "Do you mean to tell me that he actually asked you to return all his gifts?"

"Not only that, he sent me a bill for 86 house calls."

That's Fortunate

A speeding motorist was stopped by a police officer.

"I'm a good friend of the mayor," pleaded the speeder.

"That's great," said the officer as he wrote the ticket. "Now he'll know I'm on the job."

Helpful

"Yes, I'll give you a job. Now sweep out the store."

"But I'm a college graduate!"

"Get a broom and I'll show you how then."

His Opinion

"Well, sir," asked the musician, "what do you think of my compositions?"

"What do I think of them?" answered the critic. "Well, they will be played when Gounod, Beethoven, and Wagner are forgotten."

"Really?"

"Yes, but not before."

A Nuisance

Woman: I want to return this parrot my husband bought me.

Shopkeeper: Doesn't it speak?

Woman: On the contrary. It never stops interrupting me.

Can't Mistake Him

Fred: What kind of fellow is Jim? I haven't met him.

Jed: Well, if you see two fellows talking anywhere and one
of them looks bored to death, the other one is bound
to be Jim.

Tough Luck

A small boy defined "mixed emotions" as a morning when TV
news tells you the school is closed because of a blizzard—and
you're in bed with the flu.

Only Once

Housewife: Has anyone offered you work?

Idle traveler: Only once, ma'am. Other than that, I've met with
nothing but kindness.

Dejected

"Elmer, why don't you play golf with Ted anymore?" asked the
wife.

"Would you play golf with a fellow who moved the ball
with his foot when you weren't watching?" he asked.

"Well, no," admitted the wife.

"And neither will Ted," replied the dejected husband.

Hard Work

A tired-looking man dragged himself through his front door
and slumped into an easy chair.

"Busy day at the office dear?" his wife asked sympathetically.

"Terrible," he sighed. "The computer broke down in the
middle of the afternoon, and we all had to think for the rest
of the day."

New Endings

Teachers at an elementary school gave their second graders the first half of various epigrams and asked them to complete the sentences. Here are some results:

"Don't count your chickens—before you cook them."

"Don't put all your eggs—in the microwave."

"All's fair in—hockey."

"People who live in glass houses—better not take off their clothes."

"If at first you don't succeed—go play."

"All work and no play—is disgusting."

"He who laughs last—didn't understand the joke."

Trouble Ahead

"And what did my little boy do today?" the working mother asked.

"I played mailman," he replied. "I delivered real letters to all the houses on the block. I found them tied with a pink ribbon in your bottom dresser drawer."

He Can't Swim

There's a story that goes back to the time before Jimmy Carter sold the *Sequoia,* the presidential yacht that used to go up and down the Potomac River. One president was so frustrated with the way he was being treated by the news media that he invited the head of the *Washington Post,* the editor, the publisher, and the reporters to go with him on the yacht. He got them on the *Sequoia,* which took off and went down the Potomac River. They were about halfway down to Mt. Vernon when the president told the captain to stop the boat and put down the gangway. The captain put down the gangway.

The president stalked down the gangway, walked out onto the water and walked twenty paces, turned around and walked back on the water, went up the gangway, climbed onto the yacht, and said, "Back to the dock."

The next day the *Washington Post* headline was "The President Can't Swim."

He Had Them

In one state that was a heavily Democratic district, the candidate was a Republican who was going to have to get a lot of Democratic votes to win.

He stood up and told the story about the Marine Chesty Puller out in the Pacific. He was calling in his report to headquarters about the enemy. He said, "The enemy is out in front of me. The enemy is on the left; the enemy is on the right; the enemy is behind me. And they are not going to get away this time."

—*Donald H. Rumsfeld, before Executives' Club of Chicago*

Correct

From a schoolboy's exam paper: "Matterhorn was a horn blown by the ancients when anything was the matter."

Helpful

Said an anxious wife as she watched her husband fishing in a bucket of water in the middle of the living room, "I'd take him to a psychiatrist, but we really need the fish."

Most of All

Sometimes a dog has toys galore, squeakers, balls, and many more; fancy collars, sweaters too, a doghouse painted red or blue. A dog needs love for health and joy, but most of all he needs a boy.

Getting Old

You wonder if you're getting old? My girl, the test is this: When people start to call you "Ma'am" who used to call you "Miss."

Why Not?

Truck stop
customer: I'll have a tough steak, cold eggs, undercooked hashbrowns, a stale sweet roll, and weak coffee.

Waitress: I can't serve you that, sir!

Customer: Why not? You did the last time I was here.

Be Careful

"John," complained the wife, "I think I should be paid for doing housework."

"Of course dear, but I only need you to come in on Fridays."

Inflation

A panhandler walked up to a man and said: "Mister, could you spare an extra money market certificate?"

The Reason

A certain husband was angry because his wife had bought a very expensive fur coat. "Why did you have to spend so much money?" he roared.

"Well, dear," confessed his contrite wife, "I guess Satan tempted me too much."

"Then why didn't you say, 'Get thee behind me, Satan'?"

"Darling, I did, but he just looked over my shoulder and said, 'Fits you real good in the back, too, dearie.'"

He Pays for the Stadium

Grouch: I hear that the football coach gets five times as much salary as the Greek professor. Isn't that quite a discrepancy?

Student: Oh, I dunno. Did you ever hear 40,000 people cheering a Greek recitation?

No One to Blame

An elderly worker on a construction project opened his lunchbox, looked in, and growled, "Cheese sandwiches! Cheese sandwiches! Always cheese sandwiches for lunch!"

A fellow worker sitting close by overheard him and asked, "Why don't you ask your wife to make some other kind?"

"Wife?" said the elderly man. "Who's married? I make these myself."

Modern Times

A modern mother and her young son were shopping in a supermarket. The child, trying to help, picked up a package and brought it to her. "No, no, honey," protested the mother, "go put it back. You have to cook that."

Adaptable

"Almost every man can find work if he uses his brains," asserted the man who had traveled a good deal. "That is, if he has the ability to adapt himself like the piano tuner I once met in the Far West.

"We were in a wild, unsettled country, and I said to him, 'Surely piano tuning can't be very lucrative here. I should not imagine that pianos were very plentiful in this region.'

" 'No, they're not,' said the piano tuner, 'but I make a pretty fair income by tightening up barbed wire fences.' "

Making It Simple

An old gentleman who didn't have a telephone wanted to order two geese from the butcher. Not wanting to go to the shop in person, he decided to write a note and let a youngster take it for him.

In composing the note, he first wrote: "Please send me two gooses." He decided that wasn't correct and tore the note up. On his second trial, he wrote, "Please send me two geeses." This, he decided, wasn't correct either.

Finally, he hit on a solution. He wrote, "Please send me a goose." After signing his name, he added a postscript: "Send another one along with it."

Not Fair

Two fishermen sitting on a bridge, their lines in the water, made a bet as to who'd catch the first fish. One got a bite and became so excited that he fell off the bridge.

"Oh, well," said the other, "if you're going to dive for them, the bet's off!"

Handling a Problem

On one occasion, John Barrymore was playing in a Broadway theater, and a very noisy person in one of the boxes was directing remarks to the stage to show that he knew Barrymore. Finally, in the middle of a scene, Barrymore walked down to the footlights and said, "Ladies and gentlemen, please excuse my friend in the box. I haven't seen him for a long time. Now you understand why!"

One Opinion

Man: Doctor, I have a corn on the bottom of my foot.

Doctor: That's lucky. You're the only one who can step on it.

Of Course Not

Doctor: You're overweight again, Mrs. Fuller. You haven't been keeping strictly to that diet I gave you.

Mrs. Fuller: Well, no, doctor. After all, I don't want to starve to death just for the sake of living a little bit longer.

No Substitute

"Sorry we don't have potted geraniums," the clerk said, and then added helpfully, "Could you use African violets?"

"No," replied the man sadly. "It was geraniums my wife told me to water while she was gone."

One Explanation

Professor: What is the difference between electricity and lightning, class?

Student: We don't have to pay for lightning.

Definitely Maybe

The boss, leaving the office, was instructing his new secretary on what to say while he was out.

"I may be back before lunch," he told her. "And then again, I may not. I may not be back until tomorrow morning."

"Yes, sir," the secretary said. "Is that definite?"

Spoke Too Soon

Cowboy: Hey, you're putting the saddle on backward!

Dude: You think you're so smart. You don't even know which way I'm going.

Too Late

The young couple had had their first quarrel, and for several hours neither would speak to the other. Finally the husband decided to give in.

"Please speak to me dear," he said. "I'll admit I was wrong and you were right."

"It won't do any good," sobbed the bride, "I've changed my mind."

Not Quite Certain

Office clerk: Please, sir, I think you're wanted on the phone.

Employer: You think! Don't you know?

Office clerk: Well, sir, the voice at the other end said, "Hello, is that you, you old idiot?"

Fatigued

Two hard-working secretaries were heard singing the blues while riding home from work on the bus. "Isn't it fierce the way we have to work these days?"

"Fierce isn't the name. Why, I typed so many letters yesterday that last night I finished my prayers with, 'Yours truly.' "

Sideways

Customer: I'll have some lamb chops and have them lean.

Waiter: Forward or backward sir?

Made Him Happy

A businessman visited his banker and asked: "Are you worried about whether I can meet my note next month?"

"Yes, I am," confessed the banker.

"Good," said the client. "That's what I pay you 10 percent for."

Just Wonderful

The sweet young woman entered a photographer's studio with a small snapshot.

"I want this enlarged," she said.

"Certainly. Would you like it mounted?" said the clerk.

"Oh, that would be lovely," replied the woman. "He'll certainly look wonderful on a horse!"

The Way It Is

The couple went into a showroom to buy one of the new compact cars. After learning the price of the automobile, the husband remonstrated: "But that's almost as much as a big car costs!"

"Well," replied the salesman brightly, "if you want economy, you've got to pay for it."

Not a Bad Idea

Perhaps the best way to curb high school dropouts would be to make a high school diploma a prerequisite for obtaining a driver's license.

Progress

The proud father and mother had given their son a bicycle and were watching him as he rode around the block.

On his first trip around he called: "Look, Mom, no hands!"

On the second trip: "Look, Mom, no feet!"

And his third time: "Look, Mom, no teeth!"

Just Remember

"Son," a father told his growing boy, "just remember one thing: I know a lot more about being young than you know about being old."

Money

Workers earn it, spendthrifts burn it, bankers lend it, women spend it, forgers fake it, taxes take it, people dying leave it, heirs receive it, thrifty people save it, misers crave it, robbers seize it, rich increase it, gamblers lose it—we could use it.

It's Easy to Make

Teacher: If I take a potato and divide it into two parts,

then into four parts, and each of the four parts
into two parts, what would I have?

Little Emily: Potato salad.

A Tree-Toad Romance

A tree toad loved a she toad that lived up in a tree; she was
a three-toed tree toad, but a two-toed tree toad was he.

The two-toed tree toad tried to win the she toad's friendly
nod, for the two-toed tree toad loved the ground that the three-
toed tree toad trod.

But vainly the two-toed tree toad tried, for he couldn't please
her whim. In her tree-toad bower, with her v-toe power, the
she toad vetoed him.   —*Sunshine Magazine*

Find the Car

"Where is my wandering boy tonight, I wonder, near or far?"
an anxious parent asks, and adds, "And also, where's the car?"

Charming—But

There's nothing quite so charming as the rows of waving corn
where farmers do their farming on a hot midsummer morn.
No sound is quite so thrilling as the whistling that is done
through constant hours of tilling, underneath a boiling sun. No
job is quite so earthy as the pushing of a plow, and nothing
seems so worthy as the tending of a cow. No picture is as pretty
as a farmer mowing hay.

My home is in the city. That's where I plan to stay.
                                        —*Sunshine Magazine*

Too Late

Backward, turn backward, O Time, in thy flight—I've just thought
of a comeback I needed last night.

Fair Enough

One morning an old-time judge in a western mining community opened court with the announcement: "Gents, I have in hand a check—a bribe you might call it—from the plaintiff for $10,000, and another from the defendant for $15,000. I propose to return $5,000 to the defendant and decide the case strictly on its merits."

That's Better

They fed the computer at the Pentagon a series of questions, and the answer came out "yes."

The admiral in charge asked the computer, "Yes—what?"

Back came the machine: "Yes, sir!"

One Too Many

"Daddy!" cried the boy.

"One more question, then," sighed the tired father.

"How far is it," inquired the tot, "between to and fro?"

Golf

"I'd move heaven and earth to break 100," announced the duffer golfer as he banged away in a sand trap.

"Try heaven," advised his partner. "I think you've already moved enough earth."

Frustrated

The joke you just told isn't funny one bit. It is pointless and dull, wholly lacking in wit. It's so old and so stale it's beginning to smell. (Besides, it's the one I was planning to tell.)

—*Sunshine Magazine*

A Tale

Fred: Have you heard the story of the peacock?

Jed: No, I haven't.

Fred: It's a beautiful tale.

Right

Teacher: Can anyone tell me what the highest form of animal life is?

Susan: Yes, the giraffe.

For Reasons of Health

"It's not that I really cheat," the golfer explained, "it's just that I play for my health, and the low score makes me feel better."

Passed His English Course

"Whom are you?" said he, for he had been to night school.

—*George Ade*

Winter

When it freezes and bloze, take care of your noze that it doesn't get froze, and wrap up your toze in warm woolen hoze. This advice, goodness knowze, was written in proze by someone who knowze the effect of cold snowze on your noze and your toze.

—*Sunshine Magazine*

Forget the Age

"You were swindled over this Rembrandt. The picture isn't 50 years old."

"I don't care about age so long as it's a genuine Rembrandt."

Must Have Been to London

"It's nice to be back from my vacation. It rained most of the time I was gone."

"It couldn't have been too bad. That's a nice tan you have."
"That's not a tan. That's rust."

Good Try

Sports car
driver: But I wasn't doing 100!

Traffic officer: Maybe not. However, I'm going to give you
                 this ticket as first prize for trying.

Not Bad

A country lad, observing a city fisherman on the bank of a
stream, asked, "How many fish ya got mister?"

"None, yet," was the reply.

"That ain't bad," observed the boy. "There was a feller
fished here for two weeks and he didn't get any more than
you got in half an hour!"

No Extra Parts

Joe didn't listen, look, or stop; they dragged his car off
to a shop.

It only took a week or two to make his car look good
as new. But though they hunted high and low, they found
no extra parts for Joe.

Correct

Jerry: John's wife always laughs at his jokes.

Judy: They must be pretty clever.

Jerry: No—she is.

Willing

Want ad: Lovely kitten desires position as companion to little
girl. Will also do light mouse work.

A Little Bragging

Two farmers were always trying to outdo each other regarding crops. One morning the first farmer said to his boy: "Go over to Smith's and borrow his crosscut saw for me. Tell him I want to cut up a pumpkin."

On returning the boy said: "Mr. Smith said he can't let you have the saw until this afternoon. He's halfway through a potato."

How About Hockey?

Teacher: Sammy, what are the four seasons?

Sammy: Football, basketball, baseball, and track.

Nothing Really Wrong

A small boy in a department store was standing near the escalator watching the moving handrail.

"Something wrong, son?" inquired a floorwalker.

"Nope," replied the boy. "Just waiting for my chewing gum to come back."

It Helps

"I drink from twelve to fifteen cups of coffee every day."

"Doesn't it keep you awake?"

"Well, it helps."

Wise Governor

On a certain island there were a garrison of marines and a garrison of bluejackets with two senior officers.

The wives of each of the officers laid claim to a special pew in the little island church, and after much dispute, in which each asserted her right, an appeal was made to the governor.

The governor accorded a patient hearing to each of the

claimants, and gave as his decision that the pew should be occupied by the elder of the two.

Ever after that, the special pew remained unoccupied.

Can't Win

Calling my wife on the telephone is a task that makes me dizzy. When the line is clear, she isn't home, and when she's home, it's busy.

Very Cautious

The young lion tamer was being interviewed on television.

"I understand your father also was a lion tamer," said the announcer.

"Yes, indeed he was," said the young man.

"And do you actually put your head in the lion's mouth?" inquired the announcer.

"I only did it once," said the young man. "To look for Dad."

Perfect Choice

"Professor," said the old grad, "now that I've made a lot of money, I wish to do something for dear old Siwash. Let's see now, in what studies did I excel?"

"In my class, sir, you slept most of the time."

"Fine! Good suggestion! I'll build a dormitory."

He Got a Weigh with It

He carefully stepped on a scale, near the end of a lingering day; a counterfeit coin he dropped in the slot and silently stole a weigh.

Honest

As the three ladies picked up the concert program, each put on a pair of glasses.

"Of course, I really need mine only for close reading," said one.

"I wear mine only when the light is poor," said the second.

The third was honest. "I rarely wear mine," she said, "except when I want to see."

Insult

As Smith was driving down a country road, a pig ran out in front of the car and was run over.

The farmer saw the accident and was understandably annoyed. He vigorously protested his loss.

Smith was apologetic and explained that he would replace the animal.

The farmer smiled wryly at Smith and said, "You flatter yourself."

Hard Question

Sunday
school teacher: The man named Lot was warned to take his wife and flee from the city, but his wife looked back and was turned to salt.

Little boy: What happened to the flea?

Couldn't Do It

Angry guide: Why didn't you shoot that tiger?

Timid hunter: He didn't have the right kind of expression on his face for a rug.

Her Wishes

Just give me a man with a million or two, or one who is handsome would happily do. A dashing young fellow is swell any day, or one who is famous would suit me okay. But if the man shortage should get any worse, go back to the very first line in this verse.

Nagging

"My husband," explained Mrs. Smith, "is an efficiency expert for a large company."

"Imagine that," said Mrs. Jones. "But tell me, what does an efficiency expert do?"

Mrs. Smith gave the matter some thought and said, "Well, I'm not sure I can describe it exactly. When I do it, he calls it nagging."

Modern Business

The new bank officer was welcoming a lady who had just opened an account. "Be assured, Madam, to us you are never merely a number. You are two digits, a dash, a letter of the alphabet, and three more digits."

Bye Bye Birdie

"I've got good news and bad news," the caddy told the novice golfer. "The good news is you got a birdie on the sixth hole."

"And the bad?" asked the golfer.

"You're playing the fifth."

Logical

An artist was spending his vacation in an out-of-the-way town. He entered the general store and asked if they carried camel's hair brushes.

"No, sir. We don't," replied the shopkeeper. "Y'see, we never have no call for them. Nobody in these parts seems to keep camels."

Quit Living Normally

The doctor examined the patient thoroughly and asked, "Have you been living a normal life?"

"Yes doctor," the patient replied.

"Well, you'll have to cut it out for a while."

Jumping to a Conclusion

The aviation instructor, having delivered a lecture on parachuting, concluded: "And if it doesn't open, and then your reserve 'chute doesn't open either—well, gentlemen, that's what is known as 'jumping to a conclusion.' "

Wrong Number

Voice (during a telephone conversation):	And tell me, how are you feeling this morning?
Answer:	Oh, just fine.
Voice:	I think I must have the wrong number!

It Depends

"Is it true," the reporter asked the explorer, "that wild animals in the jungle will not harm you if you carry a torch?"

"It all depends," said the explorer, "on how fast you carry it."

Efficient Service

Shoe department manager: "Yes, we have quite a selection of loafers. I'll see if I can get one to wait on you."

Under Oath

"What is your age?" asked the trial lawyer. "And remember, you are under oath."

"I am twenty-one and some months," the woman answered.

"How many months?"

"One hundred and eight."

Only the Teachers

A teacher described the excitement at school when classes were dismissed for vacation. "There was foot stomping, wall banging, and all sorts of rejoicing," he said.

"Real wild, eh?" said the listener.

"Yeah," said the teacher, "and that was only in the teachers' lounge."

The Next Step

Teacher's note on a report card: "Your son excels in initiative, group integration, responsiveness, and activity participation. Now he should learn to read and write."

Famous Ancestors

"Oh, yes," said an ambitious young woman. "We can trace our ancestry back to—to—well, I don't know exactly whom, but we've been descending for several centuries."

Like Most of Us

Golfer: I'm certainly not playing the game I used to play.

Disgusted caddy: What game was that sir?

Not Here

Tourist: What a quaint little village! Truly one-half of the world is ignorant of how the other half lives.

Native: Not in this village, mister. Not in this village!

Very Good

"What are those?"
    "Cranberries."

"Are they good to eat?"

"Sure, when they're cooked they make much better applesauce than prunes do."

Don't Try It

Husband: The bank has returned your check.

Wife: Isn't that just wonderful! What shall we buy with it this time?

That's Different

Suburban
resident: It's simply fine to wake up in the morning and hear the leaves whispering outside your window.

City man: It's all right to hear the leaves whisper, but I never could stand hearing the grass mown.

Got It?

The junior member of the firm went to New York to call on a customer. When he arrived, he found that he had unaccountably forgotten the customer's name. He telephoned his partner and asked, "What is our customer's name?"

The answer came back, "Jones, Joseph H. Yours is Kent, James T. Got it?"

Perfect

Overheard at a party: "They make a perfect couple. He's a pill and she's a headache."

Can't Have Everything

A man bought a canary from an animal dealer. "You're sure this bird can sing?" he asked.

"He's a grand singer."

The customer left. A week later he reappeared.

"Say! This confounded bird you sold me is lame!"

"Well, what do you want—a singer or a dancer?"

What They Want

Two college presidents were discussing their retirement plans.

"I'd like to be superintendent of an orphans' home," said the first. "No visits from parents."

"I have a better idea," said the second. "I want to be warden of a prison. No alumni reunions."

They Made a Sale

"Were there any new orders while I was out?" the store owner asked his new clerk.

"Only one," she replied. "Two men ordered me to put up my hands while they took the safe."

He Was

"What's the matter with you, Joe? You look mournful."

"That's just it. I've eaten so much I'm more'n full."

A Sad Poem

A little boy at the end of his rope, facing a towel, water, and soap.

A Poem on Time

"I haven't time!" These idle words are not exactly true, because I always find the time for things I want to do.

Hard to Explain

"Mother," said Charlie, "I'd like to ask you a question."

"Well, what is it dear?"

"When a lightning bug lightens, why doesn't it thunder?"

Didn't Do So Well

Phil: How did you come out in the pie-eating contest?

Bill: Jimmy came in first and I came in sick.

Worth Knowing

Here's a fact that's worth the knowing, so treasure and mark it well; when the mind is through with growing, then the head begins to swell.

A Real Tragedy

Of tragedies both great and small within the reach of my recall, there's none of them can even par, the first little dent in my new car.

It Did

Bill Muffet said his car couldn't skid; this monument shows that it could—and did.

It's Hard Work

The man who goes fishing on his vacation usually gets a lot of additional exercise when he gets home. He has to stretch his arms to their full length every time he meets a friend to show him the size of the fish that got away.

Just Luck

"I've got an idea," said the freshman.
    "Beginner's luck," said the sophomore.

Getting Ahead

Old friends met after a long time.
    "Are you making any progress, Joe?" one asked.

"Well, after a fashion," Joe responded. "Ten years ago I was only a cog in a wheel. But today I'm ten holes in a punch card!"

Failure of Parental Discipline

It used to be that Dad dealt Junior a stern code of discipline. Then the electric razor took away his razor strap, the furnace took away his woodshed, and tax worries took away his hair and the hairbrush. That's why youngsters are running wild today. Dad ran out of weapons.

Our Wants

As a rule a man's a fool; when it's hot he wants it cool; when it's cool he wants it hot. Always wanting what is not.

Not Easy

Little Johnnie rushed home from school one afternoon and announced to his mother that his class was going to be split into two divisions.

"I'm going to be in the top one," he explained, "and the other one's for backward readers."

"But," he added, confidentially, "we don't know who's going to be in the other one because there's not a pupil in the room who can read backward."

Very Smart Dog

When John Jones took his hunting dog out in the fields to show him off to several strangers, to his amazement the dog pointed at one of them.

"He's smarter than you think," said the man. "My name happens to be Partridge."

Little Help

Man: I want to buy a pillowcase.

Salesgirl: What size?

Man: I'm not sure, but if it'll help, I wear a size 7 hat.

Safe

Little sister: Bobby, quick, I've dropped my cookie under the table. Don't let Rover eat it!

Bobby: Don't worry. I have my foot on it.

It Takes Time

"Dad, guess what! I've got my first part in a play," enthused the budding young actor. "I play the part of a man who's been married for twenty-five years."

"That's a good start, son," replied his dad. "Just keep at it and one of these days you'll get a speaking part."

On the Rims

The little girl was telling her teacher about her baby teeth coming out. One tooth was loose and she already had lost three.

She said: "Pretty soon I'll be running on the rims."

Obvious

What flower tells you what George Washington was to his country?

Obviously, the poppy.

Making Progress

"How many fish have you caught?" asked someone, seeing an old villager fishing on the banks of a stream.

"Well, sir," replied the old fisherman thoughtfully. "If I catch this one I'm after, and then catch two more, I'll have three."

Art Objects

A cynical man was standing in front of an exhibit of modernism labeled "Art Objects."

"Well," he announced to the attendant, "I can't say I blame Art for objecting."

Smart Dad

The junior Murray had become involved in a financial tangle. In a moment of weakness he had loaned a friend $500 without getting a receipt. Then the young man found that he needed his money. In desperation he consulted his father.

The father said, "Oh, that's easy, son. Write him and say you need the $1,000 you loaned him."

Young Murray said, "You mean $500."

"I do not," said the father. "You say $1,000, and he will immediately write back that he owes you only $500. Then you will have it in writing."

OK

Parkkeeper (to
man in pond):   Hey, you! Can't you see the notice "No
                  Swimming"?

Man: I'm not swimming, I'm drowning.

Parkkeeper: Oh, that's all right then.

He Will

Onlooker: What a glorious scene. I wish I could take these
            colors home with me.

Artist: You will. You're sitting on my paint box.

No Details

One woman to another: "I won't go into all the details; in fact, I've already told you more about it than I heard myself."

Made It Difficult

The man got off a train, green in the face. A friend who met him asked him what was wrong.

"Train sickness," said the traveler. "I'm always sick when I ride backward on a train."

"Why didn't you ask the person sitting opposite you to change with you?" the friend asked.

"I thought of that," replied the traveler, "but there wasn't anybody there."

They Wanted a Duck

An American couple decided to take a little orphan girl from a refugee camp. When she arrived at their home, they showed her a neat room and a closet full of new, clean clothes and told her how much they wanted a little girl like her.

Being daily bathers themselves, they introduced the child to daily bathing. Although unaccustomed to it, the child took the vigorous soaping and scrubbing without complaint. After a week of it, she decided maybe she had had enough.

That night, immersed in a tub of hot water with her face and body smothered in suds, she looked at her new mother and said, "You folks don't want a little girl. What you want is a duck."

Easy Question

Teacher: Why do wild geese fly south in the autumn?

Pupil: Walking would take too long.

It Pays

Two men were discussing a mutual acquaintance. "Nice fellow," said one, "but have you noticed how he always lets his friends pick up the dinner bill?"

"Yes," replied the other. "He has a terrible impediment in his reach."

Salesmanship

"Grandma, were you once a little girl like me?" asked a youngster.

"Why, yes, dear," answered Grandma smiling; "why do you ask?"

"Then," continued the little girl, "I suppose you know how it feels to get an ice cream cone when you don't expect it."

The Difference

The difference between a psychosis and a neurosis is this: A person with a psychosis thinks that two plus three equals four. A person with a neurosis knows that two plus two equals four, but it bothers him.

Everyone Does

An exasperated matron, being questioned by an Internal Revenue Service agent about her deductions, was heard to say: "I wish the government were half as fussy about how it spends money as it is about how I spend it!"

Music Lover

Little boy, listening to a violinist for the first time: "Mama, will we be going home as soon as the man has cut his box in two?"

Full Inventory

A motorist walked into the general store of a very small crossroads village. "I don't suppose you have anything in the shape of a tire?" he asked disdainfully.

"Sure do," drawled the man behind the counter. "Rubber bands, doughnuts, lifesavers, and jar rings."

Helpful

Jimmy and Johnny, panting and pulling on their tandem bicycle, finally reached the top of a long, steep hill.

"Whew!" gasped Jimmy. "What a climb!"

"Sure was!" agreed Johnny. "If I hadn't kept the brake on we'd have gone down backward."

He Knew

"I'm sorry, sir," said the boy learning to dive, "but I couldn't dive from the highest board. It's all of fifteen feet."

"I know, but you need to conquer your fear," the instructor answered firmly. "Supposing you were that high above the water on a sinking ship. What would you do then?"

"Wait for the ship to sink another ten feet, sir."

She Heard Daddy

Visiting a parishioner's home for Sunday dinner, the minister placed some green beans on his plate.

Intently watching, the small daughter of the family suddenly exclaimed, "Look, Daddy, he took some beans! You said he didn't know beans!"

Of Course

Teacher: How would you punctuate this sentence? "I saw a $5 bill on the street."

Student: I would make a dash after it.

It Wasn't That Easy

In a Sunday school class one day, the teacher asked if anyone in the class new who the twin boys were mentioned in the Bible.

A little boy at the end of the line raised his hand promptly.

"Who were they, Johnny?" the teacher asked.

"That's easy," said Johnny; "they were First and Second Samuel."

His Impression

A Chinese youth attending one of our colleges wrote home telling his folks about American institutions: "An American university is a vast athletic association, where, however, some studies are maintained for the benefit of the feeble-bodied."

Columbus's Objective

What was Columbus's objective when he made his first trip across the Atlantic?

To get more miles to the galleon.

So It Seems

Mother: I'm ashamed of you, Betty! Why are you whipping the kitty?

Betty: Cause he's dirty. He spits on his feet and wipes them on his face.

Be Thankful

"Thankful! What have I to be thankful for?" grumbled the sour-looking man to the sunshine spreader. "I can't even pay my bills."

"In that case," prompted the other readily, "be thankful that you aren't one of your creditors."

A Poem About Happy People

The world is so full of a number of things, most of them so chaotic, that those of us who are happy as kings, must either be boobs or psychotic.

A Poem with a Moral

Mary had a little cold, but wouldn't stay at home, and everywhere that Mary went, the cold was sure to roam.

It wandered into Molly's eyes and filled them full of tears; it jumped from there to Bobby's nose, and thence to Jimmie's ears. It painted Anna's throat bright red, and swelled poor Jennie's head; Dora had a fever, and a cough put Jack to bed.

The moral of this little tale is very quickly said—Mary could have saved a lot of pain, with just one day in bed!

Doing Well

"I hear that your son is getting on quite well."

"Oh, definitely! Only two years ago he was wearing my old suits. Now I wear his."

Not Fussy

Diner in
restaurant: Do you serve crabs here?

Waiter: Sure, we serve anyone. Sit down.

Miracle

After boasting of his prowess as a marksman, the hunter took aim on a lone duck overhead. "Watch this," he commanded his listeners.

He fired, and the bird flew on.

"My friends," he said with awe, "you are now viewing a miracle. There flies a dead duck!"

Competent

Willis: I've taken three lessons in French from a correspondence school.

Gillis: So. Could you carry on a conversation with a Frenchman?

Willis: Oh no, but I could talk to anybody else who had had three lessons.

Add Water

A boat being towed on a trailer had this name: "Instant Fun," and underneath these words: "Just add water."

Fussy

Bricklayer: I'd like to work here, but I can't find a place to park my car.

Foreman: I guess you won't do. We want to employ only bricklayers with chauffeurs.

Be Careful

The teacher asked a class, discussing the North American Indian, if anyone could tell what the leaders of the tribes were called.

"Chiefs," said a little girl.

"Correct," said the teacher. "And what were the women called?"

A little lad answered promptly, "Mischiefs."

Simply Stated

An economist spoke on the whys and wherefores of our economic system. He spoke for an hour and covered the subject well. Following him, the chairman said:

"Ladies and gentlemen, what our speaker has been telling you is that if your outgo exceeds your income, then your upkeep will be your downfall."

Self-Taught

Very few men are wise by their own counsel, or learned by

their own teaching; for he that was only taught by himself had a fool to his master.   —*Ben Jonson*

One Thing Remains

All the good maxims have been written. It only remains to put them into practice.   —*Blaise Pascal*

Mike Is in Trouble

"$200 for painting the garage! Say, I wouldn't pay Michelangelo that much to paint it."

"Listen, man, if that Mike what's his name paints it for a cent less, we'll picket yer place!"

Not a Total Loss

Mountain guide: "Don't go too near the edge of that precipice; it's dangerous. But if you do fall, remember to look to the left. You'll get a wonderful view."

He Knew

A tourist was visiting New Mexico. While gazing at the dinosaur bones that were all over the place, he met an old Indian who acted as an official guide.

"How old are these bones?" the tourist asked.

"Exactly 100 million and 3 years old," the Indian replied.

"How can you be so definite?" the tourist asked.

"Oh," replied the Indian, "a geologist told me they were 100 million years old, and that was exactly 3 years ago."

Sorry

A man in a restaurant was having trouble cutting his steak. No matter how much pressure he exerted or how much he jabbed at it, he got no results. Finally, he called the waiter. "You'll have to take this back and bring me another."

"Sorry, sir," said the waiter after closely examining the steak. "I can't take it back. I'm afraid you've bent it."

Did His Best

Neighbor: You have a nice collection of books, but it seems to me you ought to have more shelves.

Second neighbor: Yes, I know, but no one ever lends me any shelves.

It Helped

"I beg your pardon," said the man returning to his seat in the theater, "but did I step on your toes when I left?"

"You certainly did," came the reply.

"Good. I'm in the right row."

Hard Luck

Uncle: Hello my boy. You're not looking very happy. What's the matter?

Small nephew: Aunt Rose said I could eat as many cookies as I wanted—and I can't.

He Made the Team

The coach was always exercising his football players' minds by asking them what they would do under such and such conditions during an important game.

Walking the sideline one day, he stopped where Johnny was sitting and asked, "Johnny, if it were third down and 25 yards to go, and we were on our own 45-yard line, what would you do?"

"I'd move to the other end of the bench so I could see the play better," confessed Johnny.

Young Businessman

"Why do ducks dive?" the teacher asked the class.

"I know," said Tim, glancing at his notes, "to liquidate their bills."

The Smaller Ones

"Willie," said the teacher, "can you name the principal river of Egypt?"

"It's the Nile."

"That's right. Now can you tell me the names of some of the smaller tributaries?"

Willie hesitated, then smiled. "The juveniles!"

Executive Responsibilities

"My brother's an aquatic engineer in a big restaurant."

"What's that?"

"He's in charge of the dishwashing there."

Pay No Attention

A motorist was driving in the country when suddenly his car stopped. He got out and was checking the spark plugs when an old horse trotted up the road.

The horse said, "Better check the gas line," and trotted on.

The motorist was so frightened that he ran to the nearest farmhouse and told the farmer what had happened.

"Was it an old horse with a flopping ear?" the farmer asked.

"Yes! Yes!" cried the frightened man.

"Well, don't pay any attention to him," replied the farmer. "He doesn't know much about cars."

Musical Youngster

Little Doris was lying on her back on the floor singing away.

A little later, when her mother came into the room again, Doris was on her stomach, still singing lustily.

"Playing a game, Doris?" asked mother.

"Yes," replied Doris seriously, "I'm a record, and I've just turned myself over."

Not Easy

An elderly lady zoomed past a state trooper who was cruising along at a nominal speed. He gave chase, and when he had brought her to a stop he asked for her driver's license.

The woman looked at him sharply. "Young man," she said, "how can I be expected to show you my driver's license when you people keep taking it away?"

Very Bright

A golf pro, employed by a club to give lessons, was approached by two smarties. "Do you want to learn to play golf?" the pro asked them.

"Not me," said one, "it's Bill here. He wants to learn. I learned yesterday."

Helpful

Neighbor: You say your son gets on your nerves? Why not buy him a bicycle?

Dad: Do you think that would improve his behavior?

Neighbor: No, but it would spread it over a wider area!

Not Broke

The young lady told her friend that she was going to marry a rather eccentric millionaire.

"But," her friend said, "everyone thinks he's a little bit cracked."

"He may be cracked," the young lady said, "but he certainly isn't broke."

In Real Trouble

He rushed in the door exclaiming loudly, "Darling, I'm ruined. I've lost my job. I'm bankrupt. I haven't a cent."

His girl said soothingly, "Don't worry, sweetheart, I'll always love you—even if I never see you again."

Forget It

Smart son: Dad, I just siphoned a couple of gallons of gas out of your car for my old bus. It's okay, isn't it?

Smarter father: Sure, it's okay, son. I bought that gas with your allowance for next week. So run along and have a good time.

Shrewd Observations

The famous detective arrived on the scene.

"Heavens," he said, "this is more serious than I thought—the window is broken on both sides."

When We Know We Know

We used to think we knew we knew, but now we must confess, the more we know we know we know, we know we know the less.

How About Those Visitors?

Little drops of water, little grains of sand, make the summer cottage more than I can stand.

That Explains It?

"Why don't you make love to me like that?" She nudged her husband in the movie during a love scene.

"Do you realize how much he is paid for that?" he countered.

Real Handicap

I cannot sing the old songs that memories gently bring. I cannot sing the old songs—because I cannot sing!

Thoroughly Satisfied

Worried over what to get his girl for a birthday present, the teenaged boy asked, "Mom, if you were going to be sixteen tomorrow, what would you want?"

Mother, with a faraway look in her eyes, replied: "Not another thing, son, not another thing."

Good Question

One little boy to another, as they watched the escalator going down: "What happens when the basement gets full of steps?"

He Had Him There

"Remember, son," said the father, trying to teach a lesson, "a job well done need never be done again."

"What about mowing the lawn?" asked the skeptical boy.

Not Intentional

A man was chatting with a business acquaintance at lunch. "We're a nonprofit organization," he said. "We didn't mean to be, but we are."

Golf

I think that I shall never see a hazard tougher than a tree — a tree o'er which my ball must fly if on the green it is to lie; a tree whose leafy arms extend to kill the mashie shot I send; a tree that stands in silence there, while angry golfers race and swear. Niblicks are made for fools like me, who cannot even miss a tree!

A Soothing Poem on Debt

Rock-a-bye baby, why do you fret; are you aware of the national debt? Father has gone 'round the corner to vote millions in bonds for his snookums to tote. Are you suspicious? Sleep while you can; you can squirm later, dear, when you're a man.

It's Not Easy

Some men smile in the evening; some men smile at dawn. But the man worthwhile is the man who can smile when his two front teeth are gone.

Doing Things

There are many ways of doing things, a casual glance discloses; some folks turn up their sleeves at work, and some turn up their noses.

A Poem on Love

Slippery ice, very thin; pretty girl tumbled in. Saw a boy upon the bank—gave a shriek, and then she sank. Boy on bank heard her shout, jumped right in—helped her out. Now he's hers—very nice; but she had to break the ice.

Fiction

A former traveling man says he enjoys reading volumes on history, politics, and biography. For fictional material, he just skims through a few old expense books.

Wanted to Know Them

A mild little man walked into an income tax inspector's office, sat down, and beamed at everyone.

"What can we do for you?" the inspector asked.

"Nothing, thank you," replied the little man. "I just wanted to meet the people I'm working for."

He Knew It

Suitor: Well, Junior, your sister and I are going to be married. How's that for a piece of news?

Junior: Shucks! You just finding that out?

Poem with a New Idea

A lady who lived in East Sheen was notoriously stingy and mean. "If a sandwich," she said, "had but one piece of bread, there'd be no need for meat in between."

How Do You Test?

New executive's slogan: "If you don't have ulcers, you're not carrying your share of the load."

Pretty Bad Story

"Hey, what time is it by your watch?"

"Quarter to."

"Quarter to what?"

"I don't know—times got so bad I had to lay off one of the hands."

It's Wonderful

The village jokester was strutting about in a new suit of clothes. "This is a wonderful suit I'm wearing," he boasted.

"It looks like an ordinary piece of goods to me," ventured a crony.

"What I mean is," the jokester continued, "the wool was grown in Australia, the cloth was woven in New England, the thread was made in Britain, the suit was made in New York, and the store I bought it from is in San Francisco."

"What's so wonderful about that?"

"Isn't it wonderful so many people can make a living out of something I haven't paid for?"

Hold It

A doctor and a lawyer were in a bitter dispute. The doctor said, "A little bird told me what kind of a lawyer you are—'cheep, cheep.' "

To which the lawyer retorted, "Well, a little duck told me what kind of a doctor you are."

Unusual Case

Then there was the unusual case of the lad who was actually arrested for borrowing money. It seems he had to knock his victim down three times before he could borrow it.

Is That Clear?

The immigration officer demanded: "Name?"

"Sneeze," replied the Chinese proudly.

The official looked hard at him. "Is that your Chinese name?"

"No, Melican name," answered the Oriental blandly.

"Then let's have your native name."

"Ah Choo."

School Exams Are Funny

Read the following answers:

William Tell invented the telephone.

In mathematics, Persia gave us the dismal system.

Chemistry is the study of how a thing that is busted gets together under certain situations, and how them that's together gets separated.

A circle is a round line with no kinks in it, joined up so as not to show where it began.

To keep milk from turning sour, keep it in the cow.

Universal suffrage was when the whole universe was made to suffer.

Savages are people who can't know what wrong is until missionaries show them.

Under Her Direction

A woman never really makes a fool of a man—she merely directs the performance.

Be Careful

A witty driver was speeding through traffic. He soon found himself stopped by an officer of the law. "Look here," the policeman growled; "where's the fire?"

"What are you worrying about?" the speeder countered; "you're no fireman!"

Found at Last

Diogenes met a war veteran. "What were you in the war?" he asked.

"A private," the old soldier answered.

And Diogenes blew out his lamp and went home.

Particular

The car stalled at the corner, and the traffic light changed red, yellow, green; red, yellow, green; etc. The polite policeman stepped up beside the car and asked: "What's the matter; ain't we got any colors you like?"

Only an E

The credit department of an Eastern concern asked for a rating on a small Midwestern firm. The reply read: "Note good for any amount." A substantial deal was consummated, when it was discovered the reply should have read: "Not good for any amount." —*Union Oil Bulletin*

Right or Wrong?

Student: "The four seasons are pepper, salt, mustard, and vinegar."

Less Than Nothing

Many a man in these days has a deficit, and very often he does not know that he has it. A deficit is a very peculiar thing to have. It's what you've got when you haven't as much as you had when you had nothing.

History!

American boy (3,000 A.D.): "What was the origin of the Fourth of July celebration?"

Professor: "Its origin is buried in antiquity. One authority is of the opinion that it was on July 4 that Noah landed with his *Mayflower,* and his sons—Shem, Ham, and Japheth—set off fireworks in honor of the event, the fireworks being furnished by Solomon, Queen Elizabeth, and the Boston Tea Party. On the contrary, another authority holds that the festival is purely a civic one, dating from the time St. Patrick drove the snakes out of New York."

Absolutely Necessary

A small boy at the zoo asked why the giraffe had such a long neck. "Well, you see," said the keeper gravely, "the giraffe's head is so far removed from his body that a long neck is absolutely necessary."

He Was Caught

"I got a ticket last Friday because I was driving too slow."

"A ticket because you were driving too slow?"

"Yes. The cop caught me."

Learned Nothin'

Little Tommy had spent his first day in school. Mother was anxious to know how he had got on. "What did you learn dear?" she asked.

"Didn't learn nothin'," came the reply.

"Well, then, what did you do?"

"Didn't do nothin'. A woman wanted to know how to spell 'dog,' an' I told 'er, that's all."

Written by a Bureaucrat

A shoe-shining parlor has the following sign: "Pedal habiliments artistically lubricated and illuminated with ambidextrous facility for the infinitesimal remuneration of $1 per operator."

It's OK

"Son, you're always at the bottom of the class."

"That's all right, Dad, they teach the same things at both ends."

Not Worried

Johnny, very sick, refused to take his medicine. His mother was despairing.

She said, "You may die."

"Cheer up," said Johnny. "Daddy will be home soon and he'll make me take it."

Bright Lad

Teacher: Who can use the word "income" in a sentence?

Boy: I opened the door and income my cat.

Radio Announcement Blunders

"Go to Smith's Shoe Store. There you can be fitted by expert salespeople in all widths and sizes."

"Anyone who listens to me has had occasion to use aspirin."

"Small children with families admitted free."

"It is best to bake a custard standing in a pan of water."

How to Win a Suit

Said the attorney, retained by the farmer to sue the railroad for the killing of twenty-four hogs:

"Twenty-four hogs, gentlemen. Just think! Twenty-four—twice the number there are in the jury box."

Don't Be a Goop

The Goops they lick their fingers,
And the Goops they lick their knives;
They spill their broth
On the table cloth
And they lead untidy lives.   —*Gellett Burgess*

In Detail

"What will you have with your permanent?" asked the beauty shop attendant.

"The inside story of the Smith divorce," replied Mrs. McGossip.

An Old One

"How will you have your beard trimmed?" the barber asked.
"In silence," replied the general.

Just Nonsense

'Tis midnight, and the setting sun
Is slowly rising in the west;
The rapid rivers slowly run,
The frog is on his downy nest.
The pensive goat and sportive cow,
Hilarious, leap from bough to bough.   —*Anonymous*

More Nonsense

There was a young lady named Bright,

Who could travel much faster than light.
She started one day
In a relative way,
And came back the previous night.

Something's Wrong

A teenager was discussing her report card. "No wonder Jean always gets an A in French," she observed. "Her father and mother speak French at the table."

"If that's the case," her boyfriend said, "I ought to get an A in geometry. My parents talk in circles!"

How to Get Nothing for Something

Bet on the horses or on any sure thing.

Easy to Find

The department store engaged an efficiency expert whose obsession was to move the departments to different parts of the store every day. One day a section would be on the top floor, the next it would be in the basement, and on the third it would be placed where the restaurant had been.

After three weeks of this, an elderly woman approached a harassed floorwalker and asked him if he could tell her where the draperies department was.

"No, madam," he said wearily, "but if you'll stand here for a few minutes, I'm sure you'll see it go by."

Don't Stop

"With a car like that, my advice is to keep it moving," instructed the mechanic.

"Why?" asked the owner.

"If you ever stop, the cops will think it's an accident."

He Will Know

Rooney: Who is your wife going to vote for?

Looney: Whoever I vote for.

Rooney: Who are you going to vote for?

Looney: She hasn't decided yet.

Also a Computer

In these times, when a man says the world owes him a living, he means to include an automobile, television, and radio.

Winter

The class was asked to write a composition on "Winter." The following was turned in by the lad who usually stood at the foot of his class:

"Winter is the coldest season in the year because it comes in winter mostly. In some countries winter comes in summer, and then it is very pleasant. I wish winter come in summer in this country then we could go skating barefooted, we could snowball without giting our fingers cold, and men who go out slay-riding wouldn't halve to stop at every tavern as they do now. It snows more in winter than any other season. A wickit boy took my skates and ran off with them and I couldn't catch him. Mother says judgment will overtake him. Well, if judgment dose he will halve to be pretty lively in his legs for that boy can run buly. Now I will stop."

A Famous Limerick

A fly and a flea in a flue
Were imprisoned, so what could they do?
    Said the fly, "Let us flee!"
    "Let us fly!" said the flee,
So they flew through a flaw in the flue.

Another Limerick

> There was a young fellow named Fisher,
> Who was fishing for fish in a fissure,
> When a cod, with a grin,
> Pulled the fisherman in;
> Now they're fishing the fissure for Fisher.

The New Model

When people's cars get old and worn, and then begin to toddle, they go somewhere and trade them in, and get the latest model.

Now, I have very often thought that when my joints get achy, and when my hair has all turned gray, and knees are rather shaky; and when the onward march of time has left me rather feeble, how nice 'twould be to find a firm that deals in worn-out people.

How nice 'twould be, when feet give out, or one has dented livers, if one could go and get new parts, just like we do for flivvers. And when my form is bent with age, and gets to looking shoddy, how nice 'twould be to trade it in, and get a brand new model! —*Sunshine Magazine*

Cancel My Order

"What you eat tells what you are," said the lunch counter philosopher. Whereupon a meek little man, sitting a few stools away, called to the waitress, "Cancel my order for shrimp salad."

A Vacation

Says Hig: "A vacation is a succession of 2s. It consists of 2 weeks, which are 2 short. Afterward, you are 2 tired 2 return 2 work and 2 broke not 2."

It Wasn't Easy

A teacher told a small boy to form a sentence using the words "defeat," "defense," and "detail." After thinking a while, the boy handed this in: "De feet of de cat went over de fence before de tail."

What the Schoolboy Thought

Trigonometry is having three wives at one time.

Where Do Babies Come From?

What brings babies? The stork. It has the biggest bill.

Inevitable

Many famous persons sooner or later write their alibiography.

Strange

Teacher: What is the meaning of fat chance?

Student: It means you have a slim chance.

Is It Different Now?

The opera was "Rigoletto," and the scene had Rigoletto tearing his hair and showing a great deal of anguish because of Gilda's betrayal.

Two bobby-soxers were intensely watching the scene. When it ended, one of them turned to the other and asked, "Why is he making such a fuss?"

"Goodness, don't you know anything?" explained her friend; "in those days it was a sin."

Farm Life

A government "expert" conducting an inspection asked a veteran farmer what time he got up to go to work.

"Son," came the reply, "I don't have to go to work. I wake up in the morning surrounded by it."

No Salesman Will Call

Beggar soliciting contributions on the street: "It's just a one-shot contribution, sir. No follow-up phone calls. No monthly pledges to meet."

Where Else

A shopper reported to security that someone had taken $30 worth of groceries from her car. "Did you have them inside the car or the trunk?" the investigator asked.

"No, of course not. I had them in the glove compartment."

Simpler

Beryl Pfizer said, "I write down everything I want to remember. That way, instead of spending a lot of time trying to remember what it is I wrote down, I spend the time looking for the paper I wrote it down on."

They Sound That Way

The music publisher was talking about a new song to his promotion manager: "I've never heard such corny lyrics, such simpering sentimentality, such repetitious, uninspired melody. I'm sure we've got a big hit on our hands."

Modern

The modern young mother was reading a bedtime story to her littlest: "Then Baby Bear said, 'And somebody's been watching my little seven-inch TV set—and didn't even turn it off!' "

It Wasn't Easy

"So, your son now drives a car. How long did it take him to learn?"

"About two-and-a-half cars," replied the father sadly.

Hire Her

A minister, interviewing a woman who was applying for a church staff position, read her application and said, "I see your birthday is April 12. What year?"

Her simple reply was, "Every year."

Is This Really a Good Idea?

A certain congressman, while on his way to his office every morning, used to drop a dollar bill near the building's entrance.

"What's the big idea?" someone once asked.

"Oh," smiled the congressman, "somebody is sure to find it and be happy the rest of the day."

Hard to Explain

Why is it that the wrong number on a telephone is never busy when you call?

It's Easy

"There's one thing I don't understand," the passenger said to the pilot on the night flight. "How do you fly in the dark?"

"Well," answered the pilot, "there's a light on the left wing, a light on the right wing, and a light on the tail. All I have to do is keep the plane between the lights."

A New Explanation

The owner of a service station was complaining to an employee about his habitual tardiness. "It's funny," he said, "you're always late and you live right across the street. Now Steve Smith, who lives two miles away, is always on time."

"There's nothing funny about it," said the man. "If Steve is late in the morning, he can hurry, but if I'm late, I'm here."

Next Question

Teacher: Ginny, can you give me a definition of a volcano?

Ginny: A volcano is a mountain with the hiccups.

He Couldn't Get It

Mother: Johnny, did you get the loaf of bread I sent you out for?

Johnny: No, Mother, the store was closed.

Mother: Store closed? It couldn't be, this time of the day. Did you try the door?

Johnny: No, I didn't try the door 'cause I saw a sign on the window that said, "Home cooking."

Naturally

Two health food devotees were discussing food preferences.

"I never eat any food with additives or preservatives and I avoid fruits and vegetables that have been sprayed. I do not eat meat or poultry that has been fattened on chemical feed," said the first one.

"How do you feel?" asked his friend.

"Hungry!"

Odd Ads

The following advertisements were picked up from newspapers here and there.

Lost: Green fountain pen by a man full of red ink.

Special sale of apples and and chestnuts. Come in the morning. The early bird gets the worm.

Wanted: Small furnished apartment by a couple with no children until March 1.

Lost: Gold watch by a man with a cracked face.

Wanted: Man with horse sense to drive a motor truck.

Lost: A $5 bill by a working woman tied in a knot.

Wanted: Farm housekeeper who can milk cows, to keep house for one.

Notice: Anyone found near my chicken house at night will be found there the next morning.

Don't Try to Be Cute

Cafe patron: Why do you serve your customers instant coffee?

Owner: So they won't have grounds for complaint.

A Good President

When asked how he felt about LSD, the old-timer replied: "I think he was a very good president."

Overtime

The personnel manager was interviewing a man for a job. "How long did you work in the other place?"

"Sixty-five years."

"Sixty-five years?" exclaimed the manager. "How old are you?"

"I'm forty."

"Tell me, how could you work sixty-five years when you're only forty years old?"

"Overtime."

Life

Oh, yes, each man spoils the one he loves, and gratifies her wishes—the rich man showers her with gifts, while the poor man does the dishes!

Only One

"Did anyone in your family ever make a brilliant marriage?"
    "Only my wife."

Unusual

The long-winded lecturer had been holding forth for over an hour, except for brief pauses from time to time to gulp a drink of water. Finally, during one such pause, an old farmer in the audience leaned toward his neighbor and announced in a loud whisper: "First time I ever saw a windmill run by water."

It Seems That Way

It is unfortunate that so many people seek something for nothing. It is even more unfortunate that they are getting it.

They Point and Grin

Lives of ancestors remind us, we give photos to our kin, and departing leave behind us relatives who point and grin.

You Have to Be Careful

A small town is the place where one always looks around to see if anyone is related to the fellow about whom he is about to make an unkind remark.

Seems Correct

When asked to describe steel wool, a freshman in an engineering class said he thought it was the fleece of a hydraulic ram.

Of Course

The pupil was asked to paraphrase the sentence: "He was bent on seeing her."
He wrote: "The sight of her doubled him up."

No! No!

No, no, little freshie, a paradox isn't a pair of M.D.s.

Logical

There is a young lady in Indiana whose name is Adeline Moore. But they call her "Postscript."

Two Against Many

Stepping out between acts at the first production of one of his plays, the late George Bernard Shaw said to the audience, "What do you think of it?"
This startled everybody for a few moments, but presently a voice in the pit cried, "Rotten!"
Shaw made a bow and melted the house with one of his Irish smiles. "My friend," he said, shrugging his shoulders, and indicating the audience in front, "I quite agree with you, but what are two against so many?"

Not Long

Two small-towners were sitting on the front porch of a general store when a city slicker drove up in a flashy convertible. "Hey, you," yelled the driver, "how long has this town been dead?"
"Can't be long," drawled one of the natives, "you're the first buzzard we've seen."

Common Experience

Many a wife has helped her husband to the top of the ladder—and left him there while she tried to make up her mind whether the picture would look better there, or somewhere else.

Strategy

A woman turned sweetly to the woman near her as a seat on the crowded bus was vacated. "You sit down," she said; "you're older than I am."

The other glared. "Indeed I am not older than you! Sit down yourself!" she expostulated louder than necessary.

The first lady sat down, smiling comfortably to herself. Several blocks later she leaned toward her seatmate and confided quietly: "That remark gets me a seat every time."

Time to Change Pitchers

A young lady who had never seen a game of baseball attended one with her escort.

"Isn't that pitcher grand?" she said. "He hits their bats no matter how they hold them!"

Spoonerisms

(Misplaced letters or syllables in two or more words)
Half-warmed fish for half-formed wish.
—Reverend William A. Spooner
A drama critic is a man who leaves no turn unstoned.
—George Bernard Shaw

Malapropisms

(Word misused by someone attempting to appear learned)

He rode an alligator to the top of the building.

She has a nice sense of rumor.

It was a case of mistaken nonentity.

A pitcher of contentment.   *—Lipton's Iced Tea*

She picked a lawyer out of the phone book at ransom.
—Ina Kern

My husband doesn't munch words!   *—Mary Carter*

Don't cross your bridges until you've burned them.

—*Dick Bower*

He eats like a horse afire.   —*Angelina Bicos*

Expansion

After going into escrow for a larger house, the couple told their seven-year-old that they had to move because another baby was coming.

"Aw, that won't work," frowned the youngster. "He'll just follow us."

Hard Choice

Several years ago, the American existentialist philosopher Woody Allen began a graduation speech in this way: "More than any other time in history, mankind faces a crossroads. One path leads to despair and utter hopelessness. The other, to total extinction. Let us pray we have the wisdom to choose correctly."

Football Is Different

A husband came home from work and found his wife sobbing in front of the television set. "How in the world can you get worked up over the troubles of people in those soap operas day after day?" he asked.

"I suppose it's the same as your shouting and getting excited when you see men you don't even know grab a little ball and chase up and down a field with it."

Could Be

Ozone depletion and the greenhouse effect—are they trying to tell us that Chicken Little was right?

The Real Question

When Justice Oliver Wendell Holmes was in his 89th year (so the story goes), he was on a train one day and couldn't locate his ticket. The conductor recognized the distinguished jurist and told him not to worry—if he found his ticket later, he could mail it to the railroad. "You don't understand," worried Justice Holmes. "The problem isn't 'where is my ticket'; the problem is, 'where am I going?' "

Her View

A husband and wife were playing chess. "This reminds me of when we were dating," the wife said.

"We never played chess in those days, Gladys," the husband said.

"No, but even then, it took you two hours to make a move."

Valuable Information

While eating a typical dinner, the average person swallows 295 times.

An Oddity

Here is an oddity in words: Lincoln's Gettysburg Address contains 266 words; the Ten Commandments contain 297 words; the Declaration of Independence contains 300 words; and an order to reduce the price of cabbage contains 1,000 words.

Simple Question

A man at a party approached a psychiatrist and said, "Doctor, I understand that you can tell whether a person is intelligent or not by asking some very simple questions. Is that true?"

"Yes, a very simple question," the doctor said. "For example, Captain Cook made three voyages around the world and died on one of them. Which one?"

"Ah, Doc," the man said. "You know I'm no good at history."

After-Dinner Speaker

The banquet had been served, the desserts eaten, and the final cup of coffee poured. The waitresses had left the dining room. The noise level was high as the guests visited and joked with each other. Everyone was having a good time.

The program chairman whispered to the guest speaker, "Everybody is enjoying the evening. Do you think I should let them have a few more moments of fun, or would you like me to introduce you now?"

One Viewpoint

A patient in a hospital woke up after an operation and discovered that his room was dark because the shades were drawn. The nurse, noticing his confusion, said, "There was a big fire across the street and we didn't want you to think the operation had failed."

Two Donkeys Are Better

An old mountain woman was having trouble getting her donkey to pull its heavily laden cart up the hill. Seeing her plight, the village lawyer got behind the cart and pushed it up the hill and over the top.

As they all stopped to catch their breath, the woman told the lawyer, "Thanks a lot. I'd never have gotten it done with just one donkey."

Second Thought

The saleswoman watched as a teenager twirled in front of the mirror. "I adore this dress!" bubbled the girl. "It's absolutely perfect! I'll take it!"

Then the young shopper paused thoughtfully. "But in case my mother likes it, can I bring it back?"

We Can If We Have To

"Once my dog and I were hunting and my dog ran right into a bobcat three times his size. That bobcat took out after my dog and was gaining on him every jump. That dog looked over his shoulder and saw that bobcat was about to get him. He headed for one of those big cottonwoods that grow down in the river bottoms and then ran thirty feet right straight up the trunk of that tree."

The pioneer paused, looked me straight in the eye, and said with all the seriousness he could, "Young man, that dog didn't climb the tree because he could; he climbed it because he had to."

The Weather

One Nebraska farmer told me that he heard the drought was a lot tougher in North Dakota, so he planned to truck a bunch of his cows up north just so they could see how lucky they were. I was told by another farmer that the summer of 1988 was so dry that raccoons carried water to the sweet corn. And water skiing was temporarily outlawed by the Nebraska state legislature because of all the dust it kicked up.

Three Viewpoints

In Nebraska, they tell about the three brothers from Sweden who came to America to settle on the northern plains. All three Swedes died on the same day. They had asked to be cremated, so they were set on the same pyre. After one hour, the Swede from North Dakota was ashes, after two hours, the Swede from South Dakota was ashes, but after a day and a half, the Swede from Nebraska stepped out and said, "You know, another week of weather like this and there won't be much of a corn crop this year!"

Bad Weather

During the dry years of the 1920s and 1930s, the most common tale farmers told was the one about the time it was so hot that corn popped right on the stalks out in the fields. Two mules in the next field saw the popcorn on the ground, thought it was snow, and froze to death.

Baby's Name

"I'm going to call my baby Charles," said the author, "after Lamb, you know. He is such a dear little lamb."

"Oh, I'd call him William Dean," said the friend, "he Howells so much."

Being Sure

A small town is one where the folks know all the news before the paper comes out but merely take the paper to see whether or not the editor got the stories according to the way they heard them.

Real Power

A central banker in Belgium once said, "The real power I have is not to say I'll resign but to say I'll not resign."

Dangerous

Who ever heard of fat men heading a riot, or herding together in turbulent mobs? No, 'tis your lean, hungry men who are continually worrying society, and setting the whole community by the ears.   —*Washington Irving*

Popularized

Some historians say the Egyptians contributed more to civilization than any other people—they invented and popularized soap.

Real Competition

An American visitor was perturbed because his stories of the wonders of his country made little impression on his English friends. He could not seem to bring home to them the gigantic size of his state, or, for that matter, the superiority of American transportation. "You know," he said at last, "you can get into a train in the state of Texas at dawn and twenty-four hours later you'll still be in Texas."

"Ah, yes," one of his friends politely murmured, "we've got some pretty slow trains in this country too."

It Ain't Necessarily So

Sometimes what most people think is the truth "ain't necessarily so." For example, most people probably think Portland Cement comes from Portland, Oregon, or perhaps from Portland, Maine. But it doesn't come from Portland anywhere. It merely looks like Portland stone, which comes from England.

Most people also think chop suey is a Chinese dish and logically comes from China, but it doesn't. It was invented in Brooklyn, New York, and even then not by a Chinese cook but by an Italian. And the world-famous Italian dish spaghetti isn't really Italian in its origin. It was brought from China to Italy by the explorer Marco Polo.

Additionally, many people would seriously question your intelligence if you said that tomatoes, bananas, and pineapples are berries, but berries they are. —*Printopics*

Longevity

Several elderly church members were being asked what they attributed their longevity to. "And why do you think God has permitted you to reach the age of 98?" one wealthy lady was asked.

Without hesitation she answered, "I think He is testing the patience of my relatives."

True

One thing is certain and the rest is lies, smart guys don't wear loud bow ties. —*Herbert V. Prochnow*

Accidental

Alexander Graham Bell was trying to devise a hearing aid for his wife when he accidentally invented the telephone.

Money

About money, the late Mayor Edward Kelly, of Chicago, once expressed the universal feeling more pithily and brightly than all the Latin epigrams and Persian wise-cracks to be found in the books of quotations. According to Edward Dean Sullivan, Mr. Kelly, addressing the South Park Board, of which he was president, said: "Money is a strange commodity and a baffling subject. Time and again it has been proved a nonessential to happiness. It doesn't buy life, affect law, assure the respect of other men or win a place for its possessor in thinking society. I am referring, of course, to Confederate money."

—*Gilbert Seldes,* Saturday Evening Post

No Complaints

The parking lot owner called his three attendants together. "Listen boys," he said gently, "we haven't had one single complaint all week about dented fenders and banged bumpers."

Letting that sink in, he hammered his fist on the desk and shouted, "Now tell me! How can we make any money leaving that much space between cars?"

A Matter of Opinion

A woman took the little boy's berry pail into her house to measure out a quart of berries. He sat on the steps and whistled merrily while he waited for her to finish. "Come in," she said. "Aren't you afraid that if you don't watch me, I might cheat you?"

"No, ma'am, I'm not afraid, 'cause you'd be the one gettin' the worst of it."

The woman was puzzled, so he explained why he'd responded that way. "I'd just be losing some berries, but you'd be stealing."

In Writing

Little Jerry was bragging about how fast his father's car could go: "125 miles per hour, and Dad has it in writing from the highway patrol," he added.

Maybe

I always make it a point to speak grammatically. Who knows? It might become popular again.   —*Bette Davis*

Faults

Think of your own faults the first part of the night when you are awake and of the faults of others the latter part of the night when you are asleep.

He Agreed

The young man asked his father for $10 to take his girlfriend to a school dance.

"Here's the $10," his father said, "but for goodness' sake, make it go as far as you can."

And his son's quick reply was, "Dad, I'll make that $10 go so far you'll never see it again."

Did You Sign It?

One little boy couldn't seem to learn. One day the teacher asked him who signed the Declaration of Independence. The boy said he didn't know. For over a week the teacher asked him the same question each day, and still he couldn't come up with the right answer.

Finally she called the boy's parents in for a conference. "I don't know if your son can't or won't tell me who signed the Declaration of Independence," she said with concern.

"Come over here and sit down, son," the father said. "Now, I don't want you to lie to me. If you signed the crazy thing, admit it and let's get out of here."

Real Flattery

"To what do you owe your extraordinary success?" the company's top house-to-house salesman was asked.

. "To the first five words I say when a woman opens the door," he replied. "It goes like this: 'Miss, is your mother in?' "

He Isn't Reasonable

Two secretaries were chatting over lunch. "How do you like your new boss?" the first asked.

"He's all right, I guess," said her friend. "But I find that he's very prejudiced."

"You mean about women's lib and all that?" the first secretary asked.

"Oh, no, nothing like that," her friend said. "He just thinks there's only one way to spell a word."

He Got Along Well

The five-year-old boy was terribly spoiled. His grandparents knew it. The neighbors knew it. But his mother doted on him. He hardly left her side. And when he wanted anything, he either whined, cried, or threw a temper tantrum. Then came his first day of school.

When he came home from school, his mother met him at the door. "Was school all right?" she asked. "Did you get along all right? Did you cry?"

"Cry?" he asked. "No, I didn't cry, but the teacher did."

Will You Defend Me?

A man charged with robbing a sporting goods store asked for an attorney to defend him.

"I'll take your case," said the lawyer, "if you'll assure me of your innocence and pay me $500."

The client thought for a moment and then asked: "Will you defend me for $50 and a nice set of matched woods?"

In Other Words

The first grader had trouble pronouncing any word beginning with the letter R. He called a rabbit a "wabbit" and raspberry jam "waspberry" jam. To help him, his teacher gave him this sentence to study: "Robert gave Richard a rap in the ribs for roasting the rabbit so rare."

"Say it over and over," she told him, "and we'll see how well you do when you come back next Monday."

On Monday she called on him to repeat the sentence. This is what he said: "Bob gave Dick a poke in the side for not cooking the bunny long enough."

Speechless

How much time is wasted in meaningless chitchat! When the telephone was invented, someone told Thoreau that the people in Massachusetts could talk to the people in Texas. Thoreau wisely questioned, "But suppose the people in Massachusetts have nothing to say to the people in Texas?"

Tongue Twister

The world's worst tongue twister is supposedly "The sixth sick sheik's sixth sheep's sick." Don't trip over your tongue!

He Objected

The candidate began his speech by welcoming the audience and saying he was very happy to have such a dense crowd. With that, a man rose from his seat and began to leave, shouting, "Hold on there, we're not all that dense."

Silence

The man was sitting in the gutter listening to a curb. A policeman walked over and asked what he was doing. The man said, "Come on down here and listen."

The policeman got on his hands and knees and then got right back up and said, "I can't hear anything!"

"That's the way it's been all day," replied the man.

Let Him Eat Cake

A hobo asking for a handout at a farmhouse door said, "Lady, can you spare some pie or cake?" "I'm afraid not," said the lady of the house. "Wouldn't some bread and butter do?" "As a rule it would," answered the hobo, "but you see, lady, today is my birthday!"

A Gentleman

What did Oliver Herford call a man who never hurts anyone's feelings unintentionally?

Answer the Question

Voting
registration
clerk: Mister, can you read and write?

Prospective
voter: Young man, I want you to know that I have been chancellor of a university and president of Phi Beta Kappa.

Clerk: I didn't ask you that! I asked you, "Can you read and write?"

Smart Teacher

Teacher
(about to begin
a speech):   I am here...

Student heckler
(interrupting):   So am I.

Teacher: But you are not all there.

What Did You Say?

Teacher: Can you hear me?

Student: No, sir.

Teacher: If you can't hear me, how can you answer "No"?

The Way It Starts

How a family starts—it starts with a young man falling in love with a girl. No superior alternative has yet been found.

—*Winston Churchill*

Hard Times

Only in America can men drive to dinner in $15,000 cars, wearing $30 designer neckties, order $15 steaks, and complain about hard times.

It's True

The shoe salesman had shown the woman more than twenty pairs of shoes before she finally settled on the first pair she had tried on. As she was leaving the store, he said to her, "Thank you for coming. I wish I had a dozen customers like you."

One of the other clerks heard him, and when the customer had gone he said, "You told her you wished you had a dozen customers like her. Why did you say that to such an overbearing and hard-to-please person?"

"Because it's true," the salesman said. "I have a hundred like her and I wish I had only a dozen."

No Change

While shopping, two young ladies ran into each other for the first time in weeks. "It's good to see you," the first one said. "I haven't seen you since your engagement party. Have you set the date for the wedding?"

"The wedding is off," her friend said.

"What happened?" the first woman asked.

"Nothing special," her friend said. "I found that my love for him became weaker and weaker and finally disappeared."

"That's too bad," the first one said. "Did you return his ring?"

"Oh, no," her friend said. "My love for the ring is just as strong as ever."

Advice

The frantic father called the doctor late at night. "Please hurry," he said. "My twelve-year-old boy just swallowed a small ballpoint pen."

"I'll be there in about twenty minutes," the doctor said.

"What should I do until you get here?" the man wanted to know.

"Use a pencil," the doctor said.

One Qualification

Sir Winston Churchill, asked what qualifications were essential for a politician, replied: "The ability to foretell what will happen tomorrow, next month and next year—and to explain afterwards why it didn't happen."

Is That Right?

Daughter, aged 5 1/2, to daddy, who is a university lecturer on mathematical subjects:	Why must I still do arithmetic now that I'm in the second grade?
Daddy:	Do you always get them right?
Daughter (confidently):	Yes. Today we did five and I got four right and two wrong.

Too Late

In a school essay on parents, a little girl wrote: "We get our parents when they are so old it is very hard to change their habits."

Common Knowledge

A hotel guest and her six-year-old son were at the check-in desk and the clerk remarked to the mother: "You have a cute little boy there."

Immediately the dignified little boy said, coldly: "She knows."

His Opinion

When someone asked Groucho Marx to join a club, he said: "You don't think I'd join any club that would have me for a member, do you?"

He Does That Now

"Now," said the golf professional, "suppose you just go through the motions without hitting the ball."

"But," protested the pupil, "that's just the difficulty I'm trying to overcome."

A Real Problem

A bus driver said he could not stay on schedule if he had to keep on picking up passengers.

He Didn't Know

"I visited San Juan," said the man from Boston.

"Pardon me," said the westerner. "You should say 'San Huan.' In California we pronounce our J's like H's."

"I didn't know that," said the easterner. "I've been in the state only through Hune and Huly."

The Dignity of Labor

Labor raises honest sweat;
Leisure puts you into debt.
Labor gives you rye and wheat;
Leisure gives you naught to eat.
Labor makes you bed at eight;
Leisure lets you stay up late.
Labor makes you swell with pride;
Leisure makes you shrink inside.
Labor keeps you fit and prime,
But give me leisure every time.   —*Robert Bersohn*

Stairs

Here's to the man who invented stairs
And taught our feet to soar!
He was the first who ever burst
Into a second floor.

The world would be downstairs today
Had he not found the key;
So let his name go down to fame,
Whatever it may be.   —*Oliver Herford*

That Would Help

A wife to her seasick husband: "Do you want me to have the steward send up some dinner?"

Husband: "No, but I wish you'd have him take it on deck and throw it over the rail for me."

The Dromedary

The Dromedary is a cheerful bird:
I cannot say the same about the Kurd.   —*Hilaire Belloc*

Eat Here

A sign outside the cafeteria at the University of Colorado

proclaims: "Shoes are required to eat in the cafeteria."
Underneath, an undergraduate wrote: "Socks May Eat Wherever
They Feel Like."

Unintelligible

"What is your new baby brother's name?" the teacher asked
the little girl.

"I don't know," she said. "I can't understand a word he
says."

Two Prizes

Cheryl: When did you get that pretty silver medal?

Carol: I won it in a singing contest.

Cheryl: And how about that even prettier gold one?

Carol: I got that one at the same contest. They gave it to
me for stopping!

An Exception

A well-known minister received this letter:

"Dear Reverend: I know that God loves everybody, but
he never met my sister.

"Yours truly, Arnold (age 8)."

Try Again

A young man got a job as a bank teller. The first day at work
the cashier handed him a packet of crisp new bills. "Here,"
he said, "count these and see if there are one hundred."

The new employee started counting. He got up to fifty-
eight, stopped counting, and dropped the package into the cash
drawer. "No sense counting any further," he commented to the
cashier. "If it's OK so far, it's probably right all the way."

One Way to Do It

Two fathers were bragging about their children. "My daughter is brilliant," said the first father. "She was able to get her B.A. in only three years."

"That's nothing," said the other. "My daughter got a Ph.D. in only one year."

"That's impossible," said the first man. "How could she get a Ph.D. in one year?"

"She married him," his friend said with a smile.

Would Be Helpful

The eight-year-old wanted to decorate his room in the latest style, so he wrote to the state university and asked for "stickers, brochures, and pennance." A few days later he received a package from the university with this letter, "We are mailing you the brochures and stickers but would suggest that for pennance you spend an hour a day with Webster's dictionary."

Risky Question

They had been married just two weeks and he was going through the day's mail. "Honey," he said, "aren't these bills for all the clothes and things you bought before we were married?"

"Yes, they are darling," she replied sweetly. "You're not upset about it, are you?"

"Well," he retorted, "don't you think it's unfair to ask a fish to pay for the bait he was caught with?"

Obedient

The father of five children won a toy at a raffle. He called the family together to ask which one of them should receive the present.

"Who is the most obedient?" he asked. "Who never talks back to Mother? Who does everything she says without an argument?"

Five small voices answered his questions in unison: "You play with it, Daddy!"

Gone

With the orchid he sent his girl, the young man wrote a short but heartfelt note: "With all my love and most of my allowance."

The Same

"This story on 'A Dog' is exactly the same as the composition your brother wrote."

"Yes. We described the same dog."

He Needed Help

At the end of the day, one of the bank officers was closing the door when he noticed a customer outside with bundles in his arms and a perplexed look on his face, staring at the night deposit box. The officer approached him and asked if he could help.

The man turned to him and replied excitedly: "I hope so. My wife is going to be angry!"

"What happened?"

"I dropped the wrong package down the chute."

"What was in it?"

"Pork chops."

She Wanted to Be Right

She applied for a job as a stenographer and they gave her a spelling test.

"How do you spell Mississippi?" she was asked.

"The river or the state?"

Agreed

A group of friends were discussing the most frightening sounds they knew. "A groan in the dark," said one man, "when you think nobody is there."

"I'd say the sudden buzz of a rattlesnake at your feet when you don't have any boots on," said another.

An older man in the group grunted and topped them all. "A long, low whistle coming from an auto mechanic who's under the hood of your car!"

Just in Case

The teacher took his class to the zoo. When they stood before the lion's cage, one nervous child said to the teacher: "See the lion's big mouth! If the lion swallows you, what bus shall we take to get back to school without you?"

Trying to Learn

Student: What's a green worm, teacher?

Teacher: I don't know. What is it?

Student: I don't know, either—but one is on your collar.

Reminded Him of Teacher

Student: I remember the story about the donkey that you told us last year.

Teacher: It was funny, wasn't it?

Student: Very funny. I never see a donkey without thinking of you.

The Source

Mrs. Smith: Whenever I'm down in the dumps, I get myself a new hat.

Mrs. Jones: I've often wondered where you got them.

Now or Never

Oliver Wendell Holmes, the late and great U.S. Supreme Court justice, was once asked why he had taken up the difficult study of Greek at the age of ninety-four.

"Why, my good man, it's now or never."

Too Busy with Breakfast

Teenage brother: I thought I told you not to tell Mom and Dad what time I got home last night.

Sister: I didn't. I just said I was too busy fixing my breakfast to look at the clock.

Free TV

A man stopped at a motel and asked for a room.

"Do you want a $25 room or a $30 room?" asked the manager. "The $30 room comes with a free television."

It Depends

Teacher: If your mother gave you a large piece of pie and a small one and then told you to divide it with your brother, which would you give him?

Sally: You mean my little brother or my big one?

OK

"Daddy, could you give me 75 cents?" Billy asked.

"When I was your age, Billy," his father replied, "I asked for pennies."

"Okay then Dad, give me 75 pennies."

Is That Possible?

A guide, escorting a tour through a museum in London: "The Egyptian mummy in front of you is over 5,000 years old. It's possible that Moses saw it."

Tourist: "Moses saw it? When was Moses ever in London?"

On His Own

We telephoned an executive who's with one of the larger industrial enterprises. "He's out to lunch," his secretary confided, "but he won't be gone long—nobody took him."

Careful

Running into her former suitor at a party, a woman decided to snub him. "So sorry," she murmured when the hostess introduced him, "but I didn't get your name."

"I know you didn't," said the unabashed ex-suitor, "but you certainly tried."

Puzzling

A man tried to telephone a friend about two o'clock in the morning but dialed a wrong number. He said he was sorry and dialed again. The same sleepy voice answered.

"I'm sorry," the man said, "I was very careful when I dialed. I don't understand how I keep getting you."

"I don't understand it, either," the sleepy voice said. "I don't even have a telephone."

Better Then

The lieutenant received a complaint about the bread.

"Soldiers should not make a fuss about trivialities, my man," he said. "If Grant or Lee had had that bread in the Civil War, they would have eaten it with delight."

"Yes, sir," said the corporal, "but it was fresh then."

No Disclosure

The businessperson who despises being asked "Who's calling?" when placing a telephone call also dislikes having calls answered with a phone number. But everything fell into place one morning:

"211-8412," answered the secretary, who was guarding her supply of good morning greetings.

"May I speak to Mr. Abernathy?" asked the caller, slightly annoyed.

"May I tell him who's calling?" inquired the secretary.

"231-5774," came the remarkably controlled reply.

That's Extra

Husband: See, I fixed that little electrical problem that would
            have cost us a big bill if you had called an electrician.

Wife: But how come the lights go off when I turn on
            the hot water tap?

A New Explorer

A young schoolboy faced an oral exam in history and knew
that he would be asked, "Who discovered America?" He knew
that it was Christopher Columbus but was afraid he might forget
as he stood up in class, so he pinned the answer inside his
coat.

The next morning the teacher called his name, and as he
stood up, she asked the dreaded question. The boy opened the
wrong side of his coat, peeked in, and answered proudly, "J.
C. Penney."

Pretend

The little girl asked, "Daddy, why is Mommy singing?"
    "To get the baby to go to sleep."
    "Will she stop when the baby goes to sleep?"
    "Yes dear."
    "Then I wonder," said the little girl, "why the baby doesn't
just pretend to be asleep."

Only Licks Them

The customer in the bakery shop asked the little girl who was
helping if she ever ate the cakes. "Oh, no," replied the child.
"That would be stealing. I just lick them!"

Usually True

    We have a nice address book,
    A book that's sure to give
    The names and the addresses
    Where people used to live.

Overdoing It

A feminist boarded a crowded subway and was offered a seat by a gentleman. As he started to rise, she refused and forced him back into his seat. He tried again with the same result. At his third try, he said very firmly, "Miss, you simply must let me get up; I'm already four stops beyond my station!"

All Wrong

Asked how he'd enjoyed his recent fishing trip with his dad, the youngster confessed that it was a disaster.

"I did absolutely everything wrong," he moaned. "I talked too loud, I used the wrong bait, I reeled in too soon—and I caught more than he did."

A Second Language

A mother mouse and her baby were scampering across a floor when they heard a noise. They hoped it was a human being, but it turned out to be the family cat.

Upon seeing the mice, the cat gave chase. Mother mouse felt a swipe and a claw.

She turned in her tracks and called out in her loudest voice, "Bow-wow!" The cat ran off.

Gathering her baby to her and catching her breath, the mother mouse explained, "Now you see the importance of a second language."

His Plan

"Well, young man," his girlfriend's father said, "you've asked for my permission to marry my daughter. Do you think you can support a family?"

"No sir, I can't," he said. "I was only planning to support your daughter. The rest of you will have to get along the best you can."

Passing Judgment

Arriving for a visit, the woman asked her small granddaughter, "Megan, how do you like your new baby brother?"

"Oh, he's all right," the child shrugged. "But there were a lot of things we needed worse."

Suicidal

A new patient confided to the psychiatrist, "I'd better tell you before we begin—I suffer from marked suicidal tendencies."

"Very interesting," nodded the psychiatrist, with his best professional nod of the head. "Under the circumstances then, I'm quite sure you wouldn't mind paying the bill in advance."

Not Easy There Either

The airline passenger was complaining about the wartime practice of drawing the curtains on airplane windows three minutes before landing and three minutes after the takeoff. About to disembark, he was grousing against this "blackout." The pilot, coming down the aisle, tapped him on the shoulder. "You think it's tough on you?" he asked. "How about me, up there in the cockpit?"

Secret to Success

Rise early.
Work late.
Strike oil!

Father Taught Him

Teacher: What is capital punishment?

Pupil (whose
father is a
businessman): It's when the government sets up business in competition with you and then takes all your profits with taxes to make up its loss.

Right Place

Customer: Waiter, I'm so hungry I could eat a horse.

Waiter: You came to the right place, sir.

He Knew How Now

"Don't worry, lady," the nurse said to the woman she was preparing for the operating room. "The doctor told me this morning that he watched an operation just like this on television last night."

When You Know

You know you are getting old when:

You reach the top of the ladder and find it leaning against the wrong wall.

You turn out the lights for economic rather than romantic reasons.

Your knees buckle and your belt won't.

A fortune teller offers to read your face rather than the lines in your hand.

You have too much room in the house and not enough in the medicine cabinet.

Making Sure

One of those high-powered, take-charge corporation executives was checking into the hospital. Barking orders left and right, he had his own way until he reached the desk of a small, mild-mannered lady. She typed the man's name on a slip of paper, stuck the paper into a plastic bracelet, and then snapped it on the man's wrist before he could react.

"What's this for?" demanded Mr. Big.

"That," replied the woman, "is so we won't give you to the wrong mother when you're ready to leave."

In a Foreign Country

The train stoppped for fifteen minutes at a large station in western Canada, and the two elderly Americans stepped out onto the platform to stretch.

"What place is this?" one of them asked a man lounging against a baggage truck.

"Saskatoon, Saskatchewan," he replied.

As they returned to the train, one whispered to the other, "Isn't this exciting? They don't speak English here."

No Improvement

When the white man discovered this country, the Indians were running it, no taxes or debt, no bureaucrats, no income tax forms. White man thought he could improve on a system like that.

Wise Teacher

It was a bright spring morning, and four high school boys decided to skip classes. Arriving after lunch, they explained to the teacher that their car had a flat tire on the way to school.

To their relief, the teacher smiled understandingly and said: "You boys missed a test this morning. Please take your seats apart from one another and get out your pencil and paper. Answer this question: 'Which tire was flat?' "

Worth $20,000

A man took a picture to an art shop for framing. At the counter, he heard the woman in front of him tell the salesclerk that she wanted a frame for a picture worth $20,000.

The clerk gasped and stammered that although the shop did not usually handle such expensive items, they would certainly do their best. The woman nodded and laid her son's college diploma on the counter.

Goes South

A man was visiting in the northern part of Michigan and was chatting with a local farmer. "It sure gets mighty cold up here in the winter. I don't see how you stand this cold weather."

"We don't try to anymore," the farmer said. "We go south for the winter."

"To Florida?" the man asked.

"No," the farmer replied, "to Ann Arbor."

Almost

A child's letter read, "Dear Aunt Sarah: The present you sent for Christmas was almost as good as the one I really wanted!"

From a Fly's Viewpoint

Two flies were resting and chatting on the ceiling. "Humans are so silly," the first fly said. "They spend all this money building a beautiful ceiling like this and then walk on the floor!"

A Full Day

A mother who had just put her little boy to bed was heard to say as she shut the door and tiptoed down the hall, "This is one more day when I worked from son-up to son-down."

Couldn't Be

"How much is 9 eggs plus 7 eggs?" asked the teacher.

Junior's hand shot up. "I think it's 18," he said.

"No! Stop guessing, Junior."

"Then it's 17," he said.

"No, Junior. It's 16!"

"That can't be," Junior argued. "You said 8 and 8 are 16."

A Government Bureau

What is the nearest thing to immortality in this world? A government bureau.

Frank

The minister had been invited for dinner. After the meal, he said, "That was a wonderful dinner. It isn't often that I eat such a dinner as we just had."

"Neither do we," the little boy next to him said honestly.

The Speed of Light

The teacher had just told his class the speed of light. "So even though the sun is about 93 million miles away," he concluded, "its light reaches us in just a little over 8 minutes. Isn't that amazing?"

"Not really," one pupil shrugged. "It's downhill all the way."

Worse

A friend once wrote Mark Twain a letter stating that he was in very bad health and concluding: "Is there anything worse than having a toothache and an earache at the same time?" The humorist wrote back: "Yes, rheumatism and St. Vitus's dance."

A Future Poet

A student asked to write a verse using the words "analyze" and "anatomy" wrote:

My analyze over the ocean,
My analyze over the sea,
My analyze over the ocean,
O, bring back my ana-to-me!   —*Herbert V. Prochnow*

Confident

What makes an economic forecaster confident? No one else knows anything about the future either.

With Apologies to Thomas Gray

> The little league pitcher homeward
>   plods his weary way,
> Tired and bushed he hits the hay,
> Hoping to win another day.   —*Herbert V. Prochnow*

Never Loses

What person never loses an argument? A traffic policeman.

Or Chariot

A couple visited the Chicago Art Institute. In the Egyptian room they gazed at a mummy, over which hung a card that had printed on it: 97 B.C.

Mary Ann: "What does that mean, Hiram?"

Hiram: "I don't rightly know, but like as not it's the number of the car that killed him."

A Geography Test

Here are the names of some communities in the continental United States you might wish to visit: Ash, Kan.; Odear, Me.; Mouth, Wash.; Skeleton, Ky.; Carpet, Tex.; Shoo, Fla.; Howdy, Miss.; Fiver, Tenn.; and Kay, Oh.

Hard to Believe

Only four automobiles were registered in the United States in 1895. In 1904, only two cars were registered in Kansas City—and these two had a collision!

Good to Have Them Home

Orville and Wilbur Wright had tried repeatedly to fly a heavier-than-air craft. Finally one December day, off the sand dunes of Kitty Hawk, they did it. They actually flew! They did what man had never done before. It was the greatest news scoop of the century. Elated, they wired their sister Katherine, "We have actually flown one hundred twenty feet. Will be home for Christmas." Hastily she ran down the street and shoved the telegram at the city editor of the local paper. "Well, well," he smiled, "isn't it nice that they will be home for Christmas."

—*Sunshine Magazine*

Books

At a dinner party, Columbia professor Raymond Weaver was queried by a bright young thing, "Mr. Weaver, have you read So-and-so's book (naming a best-seller of the moment)?" Mr. Weaver confessed he had not. "Oh, you'd better hurry up—it's been out over three months."

Mr. Weaver inquired, "My dear young lady, have you read Dante's *Divine Comedy?*" "No." "Then you'd better hurry up—it's been out over six hundred years."   —*Clifton Fadiman*

How to Dress

Wear seemly gloves; not black, nor yet too light,
And least of all the pair that once was white.

—*Oliver Wendell Holmes*

Too Much Competition

I am going to Washington as a delegation of one from the American Comedians' Association to get us some aid. No industry has been hit worse than us professional humorists. There is just too much unconscious amateur talent among our elected officials.   —*Will Rogers*

Statistics

This thing called statistics was the worst thing that was invented; it's the curse of the world. We wouldn't know how bad the others were doing if we didn't have statistics.

—Will Rogers

It Worked

There's a story that a U.S. senator once took Will Rogers to the White House to meet then-President Calvin Coolidge. The senator warned Rogers that "Coolidge never smiles."

Will replied that he could make him smile.

Inside the Oval Office, the senator said, "Will, I'd like you to meet President Coolidge."

Rogers moved a little closer to the president and said, "I'm sorry, but I didn't catch the name."

Coolidge smiled.

That Is Worse

While visiting her former hometown, Dagmar Godowsky reminisced about her father, Leopold Godowsky, the noted pianist who died in 1938. She recalled that they once attended a concert at which the pianist played very badly. As he played, Godowsky whispered to her father, "Isn't it awful how much he forgets?"

To which her father replied sadly, "What he remembers is worse."

Winston Churchill vs. Nancy Astor

In 1919, Lady Nancy Astor became the first woman ever to be elected to the British House of Commons. During a heated exchange with Winston Churchill one day in Parliament, she told him: "If you were my husband, Winston, I'd poison your coffee!"

"If you were my wife, Nancy," he replied, "I'd drink it."

A Skeptic

At the time that Robert Fulton gave the first public demonstration of his steamboat, one of those "can't be done" fellows stood in the crowd along the shore repeating, "He can't start her." Suddenly there was a belch of steam and smoke and the steamboat began to move. Startled, the man stared for a moment and then began to chant, "He can't stop her."

Higher Standard

I am different from Washington; I have a higher, grander standard of principle. Washington could not lie. I can lie, but I won't.   —*Mark Twain*

Candor

Thomas Edison hated formal dinners, which seemed stuffy to him. One night at a particularly dull gathering, he decided to sneak away and return to his laboratory.

As he was pacing back and forth near the door, waiting for an opportune moment to escape, a friend came up to him.

"It certainly is a delight to see you, Mr. Edison," he said. "What are you working on now?"

"My exit," replied the inventor.

Relativity

When a man sits with a pretty girl for an hour, it seems like a minute. But let him sit on a hot stove for a minute—and it's longer than any hour. That's relativity.   —*Albert Einstein*

Experience

We should be careful to get out of an experience only the wisdom that is in it—and stop there; lest we be like the cat that sits down on a hot stove-lid. She will never sit down on a hot stove-lid again—and that is well; but also she will never sit down on a cold one anymore.   —*Mark Twain*

It Evens Out

Things are pretty well evened up in this world. Other people's troubles are not as bad as yours, but their children are a lot worse.   —*The Farmer's Digest*

Prize Winner

> There was a young man of Devizes,
> Whose ears were of different sizes;
> The one that was small
> Was of no use at all,
> But the other won several prizes.

Expecting Too Much

Pedestrian: Sorry, my good man, but I just don't give money to men on the street.

Beggar: Do you expect me to open an office?

Chapter 2

DEFINITIONS WITH HUMOR AND WISDOM

··· *A* ···

Ability: The art of getting credit for all the home runs that somebody else hits.

— *Casey Stengel*

Abstract art: A product of the untalented, sold by the unprincipled to the utterly bewildered.

— *Al Capp*

Accomplice: One who lacks brains as well as honesty.

Actor: A man who can walk to the side of a stage, peer into the wings filled with dust, other actors, stagehands, old clothes and other claptrap, and say, "What a lovely view there is from this window."   — *Variety*

Adolescence: The awkward age when a child

is too old to say something cute and too young to say something sensible.

Adolescence: The period when children are certain they will never be as stupid as their parents.

Adolescent: One who is well informed about anything he doesn't have to study.

Adult education: What goes on in a household containing teenage children.

Advertisement: The most truthful part of a newspaper.
— *Thomas Jefferson*

Advertising: The fine art of making you think you have longed all your life for something you never heard of before.

Advertising: What you do when you can't go see somebody.
— *Fairfax Cone*

Afternoon: The part of the day spent figuring how we wasted the morning.

Afterthought: A tardy sense of prudence that prompts one to try to shut his mouth about the time he has put his foot in it.

Agriculturist: One who makes his money in town and blows it in the country.   — *Elbert Hubbard*

Alphabet: A toy for children found in books, blocks, pictures, and some soup.

Ambition: A poor excuse for not having sense enough to be lazy. — *Charlie McCarthy*

Ambulance: The shuttle between a speeding automobile and a wheelchair.

America: A land where a citizen will cross the ocean to fight for democracy—and won't cross the street to vote in a national election. — *Bill Vaughan*

America: A nation that conceives many odd inventions for getting somewhere but can think of nothing to do when it gets there. — *Will Rogers*

America: Where you buy a lifetime supply of aspirin for one dollar, and use it up in two weeks. — *John Barrymore*

American: One who gets mad when a foreigner curses the institutions he curses.

Americans: People with more time-saving devices and less time than any other people in the world. — *Thomaston Times (Georgia)*

The American way: Using instant coffee to dawdle away an hour.

Ancestor worship: The conviction that your family is better dead than alive.

Anger: Momentary madness. — *Horace*

Animals: Creatures that do not grab for more when they have enough.

Antique: An object that has made a round-trip to the attic and back.

Antique collector's song: You take the highboy and I'll take the lowboy.

Antiques: Furniture that is too old for poor folks but the right age for rich people.

Antiques: The old virtues.

Apartment: A place where you start to turn off your radio and discover you've been listening to your neighbor's.

Apologize: To repeat an insult with variations.

Appeaser: One who feeds a crocodile—hoping it will eat him last. — *Winston Churchill*

April 1: The day we are reminded of what we are the other 364. — *Mark Twain*

Argument: Something that gets better when you don't have facts.

Arithmetic: Being able to count up to twenty without taking off your shoes. — *Mickey Mouse*

Arthritis: Twinges in the hinges.

Atheist: A guy who watches a Notre Dame–SMU football game and doesn't care who wins. — *Dwight D. Eisenhower*

Atheist: A man who believes himself an accident.
— *Francis Thompson*

Atheist: One who prays when he can think of no other way out of his trouble. — *Prison Mirror*

Athlete, amateur: An athlete who is paid only in cash— not by check.

Auctioneer: One who can equally and impartially admire all schools of Art. — *Oscar Wilde*

Autobiography: An unrivaled vehicle for telling the truth about other people. — *Philip Guedalla*

Automobile: A guided missile.

Awe: Showing respect with your mouth wide open.

··· *B* ···

Baby: A perfect example of minority rule.
— *Milwaukee Journal*

Bachelor: A thing of beauty and a boy forever.
— *Helen Rowland*

Backbiter: A mosquito.

Bald: When one has less hair to comb but more face to wash.

Barber: A brilliant conversationalist who cuts hair for a sideline.

Bargain: Usually something that's so reasonable they won't take it back when you find out what's wrong with it.

Benefactor: One who returns part of his loot.

Benevolence: The distinguishing characteristic of man.
— *Mencius*

Bigamy: The only crime on the books where two rites make a wrong.   — *Bob Hope*

Birth: The beginning of death.

Birthday: Anniversary of one's birth, observed only by children.

Book, best seller: The gilded tomb of a mediocre talent.
— *Logan Pearsall Smith*

Budget: A family's attempt to live below its yearnings.

Budget: A plan that tells you what you can afford to spend but doesn't keep you from spending more.

Budget: A schedule for going into debt systematically.

Budget: Telling your money where to go instead of wondering where it went. — *C. E. Hoover*

Buffet dinner: Where the hostess doesn't have enough chairs for everybody. — *Earl Wilson*

Bureaucrat: A Democrat who holds some office that a Republican wants. — *Alben W. Barkley*

Bus driver: The person who tells them all where to get off.

Business: Something which, if you don't have any, you go out of.

Business economy: A reduction in the other fellow's salary.

Business forecaster: A person who is uncertain about the future and hazy about the present.

Businessman: An amateur gardener who does his spring digging with a golf club.

Businessman: The man to whom age brings golf instead of wisdom. — *George Bernard Shaw*

··· C ···

Candidate: A person who asks for money from the wealthy and votes from the poor to protect them from each other.

Cauliflower: A cabbage with a college education.
— *Mark Twain*

Centenarian: A person who has lived to be one hundred years old. He never smoked or he smoked all his life. He used whiskey for eighty years or he never used it. He was a vegetarian or he wasn't a vegetarian. Follow these rules carefully and you too can be a centenarian.

Chairman or toastmaster: A person who introduces a person who doesn't need an introduction.

Chairman or toastmaster: A person who introduces someone who is already well known to the audience.

Checkroom: Where the sheep are separated from the coats.

Cheerfulness: The art of concealing your true feelings.

Chef: An interior decorator.

Chicken: An egg factory.

Christian nation: One that has churches too many people stay away from on Sunday.   — *Herbert V. Prochnow*

City life: Millions of people being lonesome together.
                                        — *Henry David Thoreau*

Classic: A book which people praise and don't read.
                                        — *Mark Twain*

Class reunion: A gathering where you come to the conclusion that most of the people your own age are a lot older than you are.

Class reunion: Where everyone gets together to see who is falling apart.

Combustion: What takes place when there isn't enough goods in a store to cover the insurance. — *Herbert V. Prochnow*

Commercial: The warning you get to shut off the radio or television.

Communism: Nobody's got nothin', but everybody's workin'.
— *Fred Allen*

Community fund: An organization that puts all its begs into one askit.

Conceited person: One who mistakes a big head for greatness. — *Herbert V. Prochnow*

Conference: A long coffee break.

Congress: A body of government that does not solve problems—it just investigates them.

Conscience: A still, small voice that tells when you are about to get caught.

Contortionist: The person who invented the rumble seat.

Contortionist: The only person who can do what everyone else would like to do—pat himself on the back.

Cookbook: A volume that is full of stirring passages.

Coordinator: The person who has a desk between expeditors.

Corporation: An ingenious device for obtaining individual profit without individual responsibility.   — *Ambrose Bierce*

Courage: Ignorance of the facts.

Cow: A machine that makes it possible for people to eat grass.   — *John McNulty*

Coward: One who in a perilous emergency thinks with his legs.   — *Ambrose Bierce*

Crank: A person who insists on convincing you instead of letting you convince him.

Cravat: A $25 necktie.

Crochet: An exercise that gives women something to think about when they are talking.

Croquet: Chess with sweat.   — *Joe Laurie, Jr.*

··· *D* ···

Deficit: What you have when you don't have as much as if you had nothing.

Deluxe: Mediocre in a big way.

Dentist: A collector of old magazines.

Dentist: A person who runs a filling station.

Desk: A waste basket with drawers. — *Wall Street Journal*

Diamond: A hunk of coal that stuck to its job.

Diamond: A piece of coal that made good under pressure.

Diet: A selection of foods for people who are thick and tired of it.

Diplomacy: Telling your boss he has an open mind instead of telling him he has holes in his head.
                                        — *The Inter-County Leader*

Diplomacy: The patriotic art of lying for one's country.
                                        — *Ambrose Bierce*

Diplomat: A rabbit in a silk hat.

Diplomat: One who can yawn with his mouth closed.
                                        — *College Humor*

Discretion: When you are sure you are right and then ask your wife.

Doctor: A man who has his tonsils, adenoids, and appendix.

Draw: A term used to describe the result of a battle between a dentist and a patient.

Driver, careful: The fellow who has made the last payment on his car.

··· *E* ···

Economy: Spending money without getting any fun out of it.

Education: The transmission of civilization.
— *Will and Ariel Durant*

Efficiency: Getting someone to do a job you hate.

Egg: A day's work for a hen.

Endless: The time it takes for others to find out how wonderful you are.

Etc.:   A sign you use in writing to make people believe you know more than you do.

Etiquette: Knowing which finger to put in your mouth when you whistle for the waiter.

Executive: A person who makes a prompt decision and is sometimes right.

Executive: A person who talks golf in the office and business on the golf course.

Experience: What you get while looking for something else.

Expert: One who avoids the small errors as he sweeps to the big mistake.

Expert: A person who knows enough to complicate simple matters.

Expert: Someone who is called in at the last moment to share the blame.

··· *F* ···

Fad: Something that goes in one era and out the other.

Failure: The opportunity to begin again—more wisely.

Fanatic: One who can't change his mind and won't change the subject. — *Winston Churchill*

Flattery: Often an insult in gift wrapping.
— *Herbert V. Prochnow*

Footnote: Useless information placed where you can skip it.

Friend: A person who listens attentively while you say nothing.

Friend: Someone who doesn't believe the gossip he hears about you even if he knows it's true.

Friend: Someone who knows you well and still likes you.

··· *G* ···

Garage: An attic on a lower level.

Gentility: What is left over from rich ancestors after the money is gone. — *John Ciardi*

Gentleman: A man who helps a woman across the street even if she doesn't need help.

Goblet: A small turkey.

Golf: A game in which purple people pursue white balls over green hills.   — *Herbert V. Prochnow*

Golf: A game in which you play pool in the woods or beat around the bush.

Golf optimist: A fellow who said he made fifteen on the first hole, fourteen on the second, thirteen on the third, and then blew up.

Gossip: Something that goes in one ear and over the back fence.

Grandparent: One who knows that spanking is unnecessary.

Grapefruit: Eyewash.

Gruesome: A little taller than before.

Guitar: A hillbilly harp.

Gunpowder: A substance used to make nations friendly to each other.

··· *H* ···

Hash: A conglomeration of heterogenous incompatibles that is edible.

Headlights: What the car driver uses to blind oncoming drivers.

Helpless: The feeling you have when your goldfish is sick.

Hide and sick: A game played on a vacation cruise ship by a large number of the passengers.

Hobby: Something you get goofy about to keep from going nuts about things in general.

Hockey: Mayhem on ice.

Honesty: The greatest handicap you can have in golf.

Horse sense: Something a horse has that keeps him from betting on men.

Humility: The solid foundation of all the virtues.
— Confucius

Hunter, big game: A person who can spot a leopard.

Husband: A man of few words.

··· *I* ···

Icicle: A stiff piece of water. *— Fred Allen*

Imagination: What makes some politicians think they're statesmen.

Inflation: Being broke with a lot of money in your pocket.

Inflation: When one can live as cheaply as two.

Inflation: When you can't have your cake; dieting is when you can't eat it.

Installment buying: A way to make the months seem shorter or to make time fly.

··· *J* ···

Jack: A thing that lifts a car and also keeps it going.

Jewelry: A woman's best friend. — *Edna Ferber*

Junk: Something you throw away two weeks before you need it.

Justice: A decision in your favor. — *Harry Kaufman*

··· *K* ···

Kangaroo: Nature's initial effort to produce a cheerleader.

··· *L* ···

Lean years ahead: What all of us hope for.

Liberal: A person who feels it is his responsibility to spend the conservative's money.

Life: A do-it-yourself project.

Los Angeles: Des Moines with oranges.

··· *M* ···

Mailman: The contact man with your installment creditor.

Man: The only animal that cooks.

Man: The only animal with brains enough to find a cure for the diseases caused by his own folly.

Manager of doughnut factory: A person who has charge of the hole works.

Manners: Noises you don't make when eating soup.

Mealtime: When the children sit down to continue eating.

Middle age: That period in life when your idea of getting ahead is staying even.

Middle age: When the average person is going to begin saving next month.

Middle age: When you begin to exchange your emotions for symptoms. — *Irvin S. Cobb*

Middle age: When you want to see how long your car will last instead of how fast it will go.

Middle class: The people who live in public like the rich do—and in private like the poor do.

Money: The best substitute there is for credit.

Mystery: How the Joneses do it on that salary.

··· N ···

Naive person: Anyone who thinks you are interested when you ask how he is.

Neighbor: A person who is out of something.

Nero: A Roman who was careless with candles.

Nurses: Patient people.

··· O ···

Obstinate person: One who doesn't hold opinions; they hold him.

Old-timer: Someone who remembers when charity was a virtue, not an organization.

Operation, minor: One performed on someone else.

Optimist: A fisherman who takes a camera with him when he goes fishing.

Optimist: A person who looks forward to enjoying the scenery on a detour.

Optimist: One who laughs to forget, whereas a pessimist forgets to laugh.

Optimist: Someone who sets aside an afternoon to do Christmas shopping.

Optimist: The person who thinks he will never be a sucker again. — *Herbert V. Prochnow*

Oratory: The art of making deep sounds from the chest seem like important messages from the brain.

Organ: A large upright bagpipe.

Originality: The art of concealing your source.
— *Franklin P. Jones*

... *P* ...

Parents: Hardships of children.

Patience: The companion of wisdom. — *St. Augustine*

Patience: The quality you admire in the driver behind you but can't stand in the driver who's in front of you.

Patriot: The person who is sorry he has but one income to give to his country.

Pawnbroker: One who lives off the flat of the land.

Peace: A short period between wars.

Pessimist: A person who always says things are going to get worse.

Pessimist: A person who is happy when he is wrong.
— *Herbert V. Prochnow*

Pessimist: A person who lives with an optimist.
— *College Humor*

Philosophy: Common sense in a dress suit.

Philosophy: The system of being unhappy intelligently.

Picnic: An ant's lunch.

Playing by note: Learning to play the piano by note instead of by ear. Thirty-six payments on the note and the piano is yours to learn to play.

Plumber: A person who hangs out under people's sinks.

Poise: The ability to act so that no one suspects how ill at ease you really are.

Poise: The ability to be at ease conspicuously.

Poise: The ability to be ill at ease naturally.

Politician: A goon with the wind.   — *Bob Hope*

Possibly: No or yes in three syllables.

Praise: The sweetest of all sounds.

Prejudice: A great time-saver that enables one to form opinions without bothering to get the facts.

Pretzel: A biscuit that got lost on a detour.

Primitive artist: An amateur whose work sells.
                                          — *Grandma Moses*

Procrastination: The greatest time-saver of all.

Procrastinator: One who puts off until tomorrow the things he has already put off until today.

Proof of purchase: An empty wallet.

Prosperity: Something created by hard-working citizens for politicians to boast about.

Prosperity: Something you feel, fold, and send to the Internal Revenue Service.

Psychiatrist: Someone who, when a pretty woman enters the room, watches everyone else.

Pun: The lowest form of humor, unless you thought of it first.

··· *R* ···

Race track: A place where windows clean people.

Rare volume: A borrowed book that comes back.

Reformer: Someone who wants his conscience to be your guide.

Reindeer: Horses with hatracks.

Relative, distant: A relative who owes you money.

Relative, distant: One who can be very distant—especially when he has lots of money.

Resort: A place where people go for sunshine and fresh air and then sit indoors and play bridge all day.

Resort: A town where the inhabitants live on your vacation money until the next summer.

Retraction: To make one take back a statement. For example: A newspaper headline said, "Half of the City Council Are Crooks." The City Council demanded a retraction. The next day the headline said, "Half of the City Council Are Not Crooks."

Ringleader: The first in a large family to take a bath on Saturday night.

Road hog: A car driver who meets you more than halfway.

Rock: The kind of music no matter what notes you play, wrong sounds the same.

Rummage sale: Where you buy stuff from other people's attics to put in your own.

Runner, marathon: A person who is happy to be over the hill.

Rush hour: When you travel the shortest distance in the longest time.

··· *S* ···

Scotchman: The only golfer who wouldn't knock a golf ball out of sight.

Security: When I'm very much in love with somebody extraordinary who loves me back.   — *Shelley Winters*

Self-control: The ability to carry a credit card and not abuse it.

Silence: Having nothing to say and saying it.

Skunk: A community scenter.

Small town: A place where everybody knows whose check is good.

Smart fellow: A person who says what he thinks, provided he agrees with us.

Statesman: A politician away from home.

Statesmanship: The art of changing a nation from what it is to what it ought to be.

Suburbs: A kind of healthy grave.   — *Sydney Smith*

Success: A country retail merchant retired with a fortune of $100,000. That was success. His ability to retire with $100,000, after forty years, was due to hard work, strict attention to duty, absolute honesty, economical living, and to the recent death of his uncle, who left him $98,500.

Successful wife's motto: If at first you don't succeed, cry, cry again.

··· *T* ···

Tailor: A person who does sew-sew work.

Tax: A fine for doing all right. A fine is a tax for doing wrong.

Teacher, best: The one who makes you want to learn.

Tears: A good-bye product.

Teenager: One who is old enough to know everything.

Television: A device that permits people who haven't anything to do to watch people who can't do anything.
— *Fred Allen*

Television: Chewing gum for the eyes.
— *Frank Lloyd Wright*

Thrift: A wonderful virtue—especially in an ancestor.

Thrift: Common sense applied to spending.
— *Theodore Roosevelt*

Tomorrow: The day you are going to clean the garage.

Toot ensemble: Two hundred cars waiting for a green light at a busy intersection on a Sunday afternoon.

Torn: Ripped or tone in the South.

Tragedy: A bride without a can opener.

Triumph: Umph added to try.

... *V* ...

Vacation: When older people find out they are not as young as they feel.

Vacuum cleaner: A broom with a stomach.

Vote: When you have a chance to choose the lesser of evils.

... *W* ...

Waffle: A pancake with a nonskid tread.   — *American Boy*

War: A passion play performed by idiots.   — *Bill Corum*

Webster, Noah: The author who had the biggest vocabulary.

Wife, model: One who, when she spades the garden, picks up the fish worms and saves them for her husband.

Wife, thoughtful: One who has the steaks on when her husband returns from his fishing trip.

Wind: Weather on the go.

Woman, intelligent: One who has brains enough to tell a man how wonderful he is.

Woman's ambition: To be weighed and found wanting.

Worry: The advance interest you pay on troubles that seldom come.

Wretched: How you pronounce Richard in the South.

... Z ...

Zebra: A striped horse.

Chapter 3

E PIGRAMS, QUIPS, AND WIT

Everybody Knows This

If nobody knows the trouble you've seen, you don't live in a small town.

One Benefit

If you keep your mouth shut, you'll get credit for knowing what you aren't talking about.

But You Never Do

Wouldn't it be nice if you could go to the movies and see a picture as good as the one that's coming next week?

But It's More Fun

Just about the time a woman thinks her work is all done, she becomes a grandmother.

Expensive

Education will never become as expensive as ignorance.

It Could Be Tougher

Life is pretty tough, but just think how much tougher it would be if you couldn't sleep a third of it away.

It Seems That Way

The world gets better every day—then worse again in the evening.   —*Kin Hubbard*

Most of Us Have Tried

What you don't know makes you look pretty stupid when you try to tell it.

How to Lose Friends

The sharp tongue severs many a friendship.

Watch It!

If you have a good temper, keep it. If you have a bad temper, don't lose it.

Besides, It Helps the Companies

Faith will never die as long as color seed catalogs are printed.

No Trouble

The nice thing about a gift of money is that it's so easy to exchange.

Difficult to Find

What the kids would like is something that will separate the men from the toys.

Correct

License plate on car of retired drill sergeant: "HUP 234."

Work—a Necessity

Work is a necessity for a man. Man invented the alarm clock.
—*Pablo Picasso*

How You Know

The man who gives in when he is wrong is wise. The man who gives in when he is right is married.

Pretty Expensive

When the philosopher said, "Hitch your wagon to a star," he had no idea what the space programs would cost.

The View Changes

Somehow or other, as we get older, work seems a lot less fun, and fun seems a lot more work.

London

Sign on sharp turn: Dead Slow.

Seems Fair

Despite inflation, a penny for some people's thoughts is still a fair price.

Exhausted

The average taxpayer is the first of America's natural resources to be exhausted.

They Soon Learn

Many new fathers soon learn what it means to live in a changing world.

Generally

The only things children wear out faster than shoes are parents and teachers.

One Advantage

The world changes so fast that a person can't be wrong all the time.

It Doesn't Talk as Well

Money may talk, but today's dollar doesn't have cents enough to say very much.

It Might Be

Wouldn't it be simpler to isolate and label the few things that aren't harmful to your health?

They Can Prove It

Some people have no talent for counting calories—and they have the figures to prove it.

Don't Yell

Yelling at children is not the way to make the home a howling success.

It Goes Rapidly

About the time one learns how to make the most of life, the most of it is gone.

Not Always

There are always two sides to a question—if we aren't involved.

It Helps to Know That

Even perfect people buy pencils with erasers.

One Advantage

Keeping your chin up also keeps your mouth closed.

Not Now

We can remember when it was cheaper to park the car than to drive it.

You Are Also Intact

Stop and let the trains go by—it hardly takes a minute. Your car starts out again intact, and, better still, you're in it.

Fiction?

Politicians spin their yarns with smooth, flawless diction, but one must read between the lines to know whether it's truth or fiction.

All Her Fault

He wrecked his car, he lost his job, and yet throughout his life, he took his troubles like a man—he blamed them on his wife.

No Sale

I didn't get to buy that fancy raiment; what I thought was the price was actually just the downpayment.

It's Easy

If you are the kind of person who likes a little free newspaper publicity, just do something dumb.

Making a Good Husband

It takes two good women to make a good husband, and the first one is his mother.

It Would Be Difficult

The only man who can't change his mind is a man who hasn't got one.   —*Edward Noyes Wescott*

Making Progress

Sign on a road: If you're lost, just keep on going. You're making good time.

Every Year

We have a neighbor who is a regular churchgoer—never misses an Easter.

We Saw the Pictures

Sign in an art gallery: We hung these pictures because we couldn't find the artists.

Don't Wait

If you're going to teach your children the value of a dollar, you're going to have to do it awfully fast.

Sounds Logical

A lot of trouble in this world is caused by combining a narrow mind with a wide mouth.

Keep Out

A passerby read this notice on the gate to a farm: KEEP OUT. Guard dog is loose. Survivors will be prosecuted.

Financial Success

The secret of financial success is to spend what you have left after saving, instead of saving what you have left after spending.

The Hardest Time

Some people find that the hardest time to get any work done is between coffee breaks.

Who Writes the Biography?

Every great man nowadays has his disciples and it is always Judas who writes the biography.   —*Oscar Wilde*

Say That Again

If our boys and girls are not as good as they were when you were a child their age, it may be that they had a better mother and dad than your child has.

Experience

Experience is a great teacher. A man never wakes his second baby to see it smile.

Both Important

Wisdom is divided into two parts: (1) having a great deal to say; (2) not saying it.

Especially the Station Wagon

To live in the country, one must have the soul of a poet, the mind of a philosopher, the simple tastes of a hermit—and a good station wagon.

New Philosophy

I have a new philosophy. I'm only going to dread one day at a time. *—Charles Schulz*

How Some Drive

Some people drive as if they were anxious to have their accident quickly and get it over with.

It May

Reading made Don Quixote a gentleman, but believing what he read made him mad. *—George Bernard Shaw*

How Anger Works

It wouldn't hurt so much to become angry except that, for some reason, anger makes your mouth work faster than your mind.
—Construction Digest

Unless

The business of government is to keep the government out of business—that is, unless business needs government aid.
—Will Rogers

Lucky

It's a good thing that beauty is only skin deep, or I'd be rotten to the core. *—Phyllis Diller*

It Sounds That Way

Modern music covers a multitude of dins.

Obviously

The man who invented the alarm clock apparently didn't have children.

Difficult

It is difficult to believe that someone can differ from us and be right. —*The Woodville Leader*

Some Advice

Don't punch a fellow in the nose when he calls you a fool, unless you think he needs that additional evidence to prove he's right.

What People Prefer

People would rather be shown how valuable you are, not told.
—*Roger Babson*

Who Rules the Roost?

When it comes to home rule, Dad may be the chief executive, but Mother is usually the speaker of the house.

Seems Doubtful

If your parents didn't have any children, the chances are you won't either.

Money

Americans used to shout, "Give me liberty!" Now they just leave off the last word.

Efficiency

Someone crossed a carrier pigeon with a woodpecker—he not only carries the messages, he also knocks on the door.

It Annoys Us

Have you noticed how close some motorists drive ahead of you?

It Could Be

I have always thought of a dog lover as a dog that was in love with another dog.   —*James Thurber*

Total Stranger

He won't listen to his conscience. He doesn't want advice from a total stranger.

Well-to-Do

He looks like a million—after taxes.

Seventy Years Young

To be seventy years young is sometimes far more cheerful and hopeful than to be forty years old.   —*Oliver Wendell Holmes*

Much More

If the Founding Fathers were using the modern idiom, they would promise life, liberty, and the pursuit of happiness and much, much more.

A Hard Test

This will never be a civilized country until we spend more money for books than we do for chewing gum.   —*Elbert Hubbard*

No Better

Modern art is now being faked, but there is no proof yet that the fake is any better than the original.

The Land of Opportunity

America is still the land of opportunity—where a man can start out digging ditches and wind up behind a desk—if he doesn't mind the financial sacrifice. —*Bill Vaughan,* Kansas City Star

Not a Little

You can't explode an A-bomb a little. —*Hartford Courant*

New Books

The worst thing about new books is that they keep us from reading the old ones. —*Joseph Joubert*

What We Believe

Generally the theories we believe we call facts, and the facts we disbelieve we call theories. —*Felix Cohen*

Correct

Seeing is deceiving. It's eating that's believing. —*James Thurber*

Doubt

Even "yes" men aren't really sure these days.

Willing People

The world is full of willing people; some willing to work, the rest willing to let them. —*Robert Frost*

Difficult to See

Few people have good enough sight to see their own faults.

They Spell Better

They spell it Vinci and pronounce it Vinchy; foreigners always spell better than they pronounce.   —*Mark Twain*

And to Make a Living

Man invented work as an easy way to escape boredom.

We Suggest

If the government issues a stamp commemorating the IRS, we suggest "You moisten it with blood, sweat, and tears."

Long Conversations

The longest conversations are usually held by persons with little or nothing to say.

Don't Ask Her

Don't ask me how old I am. All I know is that they say I was born in 'tater time and they forgot whether they were digging or planting.   —*Minnie Pearl*

Two Views

There are two sides to every story: the book and the movie.

He Worked at It

An admirer once asked James Barrie how he managed to grow old so gracefully. He answered, "My dear lady, I give all my time to it."   —*Walter Winchell*

Generally

Money isn't everything—sometimes it isn't even enough.

Advice to Father

Take your boy fishing and you won't have to hunt for him.

Men

I like men to behave like men—strong and childish.

—*Françoise Sagan*

No Real Loss

The guy who talks his head off isn't losing much.

What the Years Do

Years make all persons old—a few wise.

How It Helps

The marvelous thing about a vacation is that it makes you feel good enough to go back to work and poor enough to make you have to.

Frankness

Frankness is a virtue, but too much frankness is rudeness.

—*Gotschal*

Hiking and Shopping

Men consider a fifty-mile hike physical fitness. Women call it shopping.

An Excess But

Americans seem to have an excess of everything but parking space and religion.

Worst Thing About Age

The worst thing about growing old is having to listen to a lot of advice from one's children.

What It Reveals

An autobiography usually reveals nothing bad about its writer except his memory.   —*Franklin P. Jones*

Growing Old

Growing old is like riding on a train: We seem to set still while the landscape moves by.   —*Marcelene Cox,*
Ladies' Home Journal

You Don't Need Manners

Too much of the world is run on the theory that you don't need road manners if you're a five-ton truck.

Knows All But

He knows all about art, but he doesn't know what he likes.
—*James Thurber*

The Worst Moment

The worst moment for the atheist is when he is really thankful and has nobody to thank.   —*Dante Gabriel Rossetti*

For a Good Argument

The fewer the facts, the better the argument.

Modern Artists

It is said some artists paint with one eye shut. Many modern artists shut both eyes.

The Voice of Conscience

Those who rarely hear the shrill voice of conscience seem never to miss the faint whisper of temptation.

The View Later

Enjoy yourself now. These are the good old days you are going to miss later.

Assurance

The wise husband is the one who knows he is right but always asks his wife what she thinks about it.

Taking Chances

About the time a man gets his temper under control, he goes out and plays golf again.

An Advantage

No matter how bad a child is, he's still good for an exemption on the income tax return.

Useful Advice

Cooking hint: The best way to serve spinach is to someone else.

Getting Older

A man is getting older when he is going to feel just as well as he ever did in a day or two.   —*Herbert V. Prochnow*

Sincere Flattery

No matter what other nations may say about us—immigration is still the sincerest form of flattery.   —*Town Journal*

When He Doesn't Argue

I never make the mistake of arguing with people for whose opinions I have no respect.   —*Edward Gibbon*

How People Drive

A great many people drive like tomorrow isn't worth waiting for.

It Does Happen

The best blood will sometimes get into a fool or a mosquito.
—*Austin O'Malley*

Appreciation

No one is more appreciated than the person who leaves time on the parking meter.

Unusual Country

This is the only country in the world where a man can ride in his own car to the courthouse to collect his unemployment compensation check.   —*Sioux County Capital* (Iowa)

It Always Happens

The first one to see a traffic light turn green is the second car back.

If

Most people can accept good advice gracefully—if it doesn't interfere with their plans.

Don't Hesitate

Don't hesitate to give advice. It passes the time and nobody will follow it anyway.

A Good Definition

What is an epigram? a dwarfish whole,
Its body brevity, and wit its soul.
—*Samuel Taylor Coleridge*

Overheard

I'm going to get out of debt this year if I have to mortgage my house to do it!

Not So Fickle

Notice in a public park flower garden: "Love 'em and leave 'em."

He Misses the Idea

He misses what is meant by epigram
Who thinks it only frivolous flim-flam.   —*Martial*

Sound Mind

Being of sound mind, I spent all my money before I died.

What They Don't Like

Most people are in favor of progress; it's just the changes that they don't like.

Never Welcome May Be Correct

Advice is seldom welcome; and those who want it the most always like it the least.   —*Lord Chesterfield*

How to Be Equal

Women will never be men's equals until they can sport a bald spot on top of their heads and still think they're handsome.

Prophetic

How prophetic L'Enfant was when he laid out Washington as a city that goes around in circles!   *—John Mason Brown*

Temptation

The number of times the average man says "no" to temptation is once weakly.

Seldom Think

The world seems to be full of people who speak twice before they think once.

Based on Experience

If someone offers you the world on a platter, take the platter instead.

Stubborn

Some minds are like concrete—all mixed up and permanently set.

They Seem to Be

Sometimes we think a good many politicians are close to bankruptcy.   *—Herbert V. Prochnow*

Give Them Time

Nothing's wrong with the younger generation the older generation didn't outgrow.

Even Less Popular

The only person less popular than a wise guy is a wise guy who happens to be right.

What the Computer Can Do

In a few minutes a computer can make a mistake so great that it would take many men many months to equal it.

—*Merle L. Meacham*

Even Greater

A learned blockhead is a greater blockhead than an ignorant one. —*Benjamin Franklin*

Listen Carefully

Woman chatting: I never repeat gossip, so listen closely now.

But We Don't

It wouldn't be so bad to let one's mind go blank if one always remembered to turn off the sound.

Right Time

The best time to spade the garden is right after your wife tells you to do it.

Better Off

There's nothing like the first horseback ride to make a person feel better off.

It Takes Hard Work

A person has to work himself to death to buy all those laborsaving devices these days.

A Hope

The beauty of rearing a large family is that at least one of them may not turn out like the others.

No Ancestor Worship

The huge national debt our younger generation has inherited should keep them from one indulgence: ancestor worship.

Companions

He that lieth down with dogs, shall rise up with fleas.

—Benjamin Franklin

More Fun

Living in the past is lots of fun. Besides, it's cheaper.

Tact and Truth

Some people have tact; others tell the truth.

When Egotists Meet

When two egotists meet, it is a case of an I for an I.

Two Worries

Two things worry me these days, one, that things may never get back to normal, and two, that they already have.

Minority Rule

A perfect example of minority rule is a baby in the house.

A Bad Example

George Washington set a bad example when he threw a dollar

across the Potomac. They've been throwing it away down there ever since.

The Truth

I don't care what is written about me so long as it isn't true.
—*Katharine Hepburn*

We Need the Diets

Americans have more food to eat than any other people and more diets to keep them from eating it.

Not Ambitious

Just put me on the lazy, no-account list.
—*John Nance Garner, former vice president of the United States*

Exposure

A stitch in time saves embarrassing exposure.

The Real Problem

The trouble with being a parent is that by the time you're experienced, you're usually unemployed.

The Cost

The best things in life are free. It's the worst things that are so expensive.

Can't Fool Them

If you think children don't know the value of money, try giving one a nickel.

Not Easy

A successful man is one who can earn more than his family can spend.

Seems Logical

You ain't learnin' when you're talkin'.
—*Lyndon Baines Johnson*

Not New

The ancient religions had a goat on which all the sins were placed, so blaming the Federal Reserve for a recession isn't a new idea.

One Reason

Figures don't lie—which is one reason why tailoring is so difficult.

Almost There Now

Cars are being made that will withstand harder and harder bumps. Pretty soon one will be made that will knock down a pedestrian without jarring the driver.

Good Reason

There must have been some reason nature made man's ears to stay open and his mouth to shut.

What Man's Inhumanity Does

Man's inhumanity to man makes prizefights, wars, and buffet suppers.

Optimist

We understand there are some horses that are trained to know a green light means go and a red light means stop. There may still be hope for some motorists.

No Fear

Men look back to the good old days when they had longer shirttails and could straighten up without fear.

Never Good

It may be bad to talk when your mouth is full, but it isn't too good either when your head is empty. *—Herbert V. Prochnow*

The Ten Commandments

There are no commandments harder to live by than the first ten.

You Are Never Right

There is nothing raises a man's hope more in vain than the first spring cantaloupes.

A Good Idea May Run Wild

Even a good idea may run wild in an open and empty mind.
—Herbert V. Prochnow

Or Even the Center

If Russia would keep on the right side of the road, there wouldn't be any collision.

The First Rule

The first rule of public speaking is to keep one's mouth shut when one has nothing to say. *—Herbert V. Prochnow*

Advice to Parents

Now comes the parently advice that we mustn't let our children suck their thumbs because they may need them some day.

Export Business

If you think business is a little slow, how would you like to be an American automobile salesperson in Japan?
                              —*Herbert V. Prochnow*

That's Free

Money will buy a pretty good dog but it won't buy the wag of his tail. —*Josh Billings (Henry Wheeler Shaw)*

How Erasmus Spent

When I get a little money, I buy books; and if any is left, I buy food and clothes. —*Desiderius Erasmus*

Or Helsinki

With modern jets, you can experience the thrill of having breakfast in Los Angeles, lunch in New York, dinner in London, and baggage in Rome.

Wanting Things

I do not read advertisements—I would spend all my time wanting things. —*Archbishop of Canterbury*

Hard to Explain

No one has been able to explain why a child can't walk around a puddle.

How to Analyze the Economy

When there is too much stall in installment, the boom has gone too far.   —*Herbert V. Prochnow*

One World

Every once in a while you read that some nation has shot some crooks and grafters. Guess it's one world after all.
—*Herbert V. Prochnow*

How to Get Attention

Talk to anyone about himself and he will listen without interrupting.   —*Herbert V. Prochnow*

It Doesn't Take Presence

Our experience is that presents make the heart grow fonder.
—*Herbert V. Prochnow*

Springtime in the South

   Flower
   In the crannied wall,
   I broke a leg
   To pluck you-all.   —*Herbert V. Prochnow*

Supply or Demand Side Economics

In a recession, prices are determined by the economic law of oversupply and underdemand.   —*Herbert V. Prochnow*

What's Wrong

The only thing wrong with the world is people.
—*Herbert V. Prochnow*

They All Have Budget Deficits

Every nation finds it difficult to balance a budget at the end of the sword.   —*Herbert V. Prochnow*

Not Necessary

In the great open spaces men are men, but not all of them wear cowboy hats to prove it.   —*Herbert V. Prochnow*

Interest on a Loan

Interest on a loan may be so high that if you can afford to pay it, you don't need the loan.

Hands Across the Sea

The hands across the sea idea often has a little itch in the palms.
—*Herbert V. Prochnow*

Helpful

How to figure a week's household budget now: Estimate expenses liberally, multiply by 2, then add $50.

What the Critics Say

Russia believes in the liberty of the suppress.

Strange

The busier the New York Stock Exchange is, the less time a member has to sit down, and yet the more a seat costs.

To Be Safe

If you criticize a mule, do it to his face.   —*Herbert V. Prochnow*

Optimist

Our first spring seed catalog has just arrived. We're happy to report that the present lack of confidence in the general situation hasn't affected the seed catalog artist.

Fooling Himself

The person who thinks he is fooling everyone but himself is nearsighted.

It Pays to Remember

A short speech may not be the best speech, but the best speech is a short one.

An Heir Raid

When the relatives gather to hear the will read, it reminds you of an heir raid.

It Works

There is no cure for insomnia like listening to yourself talk.

The Stork's Bill

No bird has a bill as long as the stork's.

It Helps

Poor memory has its benefits. Otherwise a person would remember the times he has been a fool.

The Difference

More money is spent on chewing gum than books. But after all, you can borrow a book.

Social Insects

An author recently wrote a book called *American Social Insects.* All of us know some he never met.

The Pedestrian

Every year is leap year for the pedestrian.

It's Different Now

In the modern family, the daughters don't live at home until after they're married.

They Tell Your Fortune

There's no fortune teller like Dun & Bradstreet.

The Reason

The reason history has to repeat itself is that no one heard it the first time.

Worth It

If you lend someone $10 and don't see him again, it may be worth it.

Or Your Rights

It pays to drive carefully and not insist on your rites.

It Is Sometimes Discouraging

The thing that is discouraging about spring is that everything seems to come back but us.

Is This Clear?

When you hear one person talk about what he does not understand to another person who doesn't understand him, that is economics.

What Bothers You

It may be your winter underwear and not your conscience that bothers you.

Observant

As Johnnie told teacher: "The siren doesn't blow for the fire. It blows for water. They've got the fire."

—*Herbert V. Prochnow*

Equal Rights

In communist countries, the women have the same freedom the men don't have.

How Could They?

Husbands don't tell their wives everything. After all, there are only twenty-four hours in a day.

The Religion Some People Want

Some people want a religion that will make them feel respectable but not require them to be.   —*Herbert V. Prochnow*

An All-Wool, Cotton, Nylon Suit

The cotton in an all-wool suit made of nylon can't feel very sheepish.   —*Herbert V. Prochnow*

He Has to Be Careful

A man never knows how careful he can be until he puts on a white summer outfit.   —*Herbert V. Prochnow*

You Can't Win

When you go back to your old hometown, you find half the people don't remember you and the other half don't know you've been away.   —*Herbert V. Prochnow*

Liars Also Figure

Figures don't lie, but a lot of lying can be done with them.
—*Herbert V. Prochnow*

Each One Writes a Book

We admire the courage of the retired generals and politicians who decide that now it can be told—at $5 a word.

Our Deficits

A federal deficit is bad, but it's comforting to have at least one thing that's permanent and unchanging.
—*Herbert V. Prochnow*

Our Debtor Half

Uncle Sam may refer to much of the world as his debtor half.

How They Get into Trouble

Many a nation now plays a loan hand.

Related

Soviet Russia and China may be brothers, but so were the James boys.   —*Herbert V. Prochnow*

Ask for More When You Start

If a woman wants a $300 dress, she ought to start yelling for a grand piano. —*Herbert V. Prochnow*

Unfortunate

Pity the person who has insomnia so bad he can't even sleep in the office.

It's Also an Asset

Every now and then you find a woman who can dish it out better than she can cook. —*Herbert V. Prochnow*

Little Conviction

It isn't how much thought went into developing television that determines how much thought now comes out of it.
—*Herbert V. Prochnow*

The Designs Are Permanent

Women's styles change far more frequently than their designs.
—*Herbert V. Prochnow*

Fortunate

No two persons are alike, and most of them are glad of it.
—*Herbert V. Prochnow*

It Depends

Whether a pedestrian gets an even break depends on just how he was hit.

As a Second Grader Wrote

Second-grade students were read a series of wise sayings and then asked to complete the sentences by filling in the missing words. Here's what one little girl wrote:

The race is not to the swift ... but to the finish line.

Haste makes ... more time.

Two heads are ... funny looking.

A stitch in time saves ... your pants.

Better late than ... missing school.

The grass is always greener ... than the cows.

Clothes make ... people decent.

It is always darkest before ... the light.

Do unto others ... like you don't do to yourself.

We have nothing to fear but ... we're still scared.

—*Olga Corsi in* Sunshine Magazine

Great Achievement

It is no great thing to be humble when you are brought low; but to be humble when you are praised is a great and rare attainment.

Not New

If at first you don't succeed, you're like everyone else.

And Intelligent

Some fellows are so farsighted that they rest before they get tired.

Very Tiresome

Doing nothing is the most tiresome job in the world because you can't quit and rest.

A Real Friend

He is the kind of a friend you can depend on—always around when he needs you.

Advice

Former Mayor LaGuardia to reporters, "Be sure you have your facts straight before you distort them."

Act Now

You cannot do a kindness too soon, because you never know how soon it will be too late.

Be Very Careful

Children should be very careful what they say. Parents are always repeating what they hear.

Similar

Young people are alike these days in many disrespects.

It Ain't Easy

Only a woman can skin a wolf and get a mink.

Right

Most people can keep a secret; it's the folks they tell it to who can't.

We're All There Now

An American can consider himself a success when it costs him more to support his government than his family.

They're Probably Happier

The reason most people know little about what's going on in the world is that this information isn't found in the comic strips.

Worth It

Much advice may be had for nothing—and usually it's worth it.

Don't Look

Where did you get the idea that swimming is good for the figure? Did you ever take a good look at a whale?

That Helps

Listening to advice may get you into trouble, but it makes the other person feel better.

It's Hard to Stop Not Working

Some persons accomplish nothing and then stop to rest.

Intuition

Intuition is what enables a woman to contradict her husband before he says anything.

We All Are

The easiest thing in the world is to convince a person that he is overworked.

He Has It

A tax collector has what it takes to take what you've got.

So Little Silence

That silence is golden may explain why there's so little of it.

Great Puzzle

One of the greatest puzzles is how the fool and his money got together in the first place.

Badly Needed

What we would like is a car you can drive to the office or store and then fold up and carry with you.

Tax Increases and Tax Cuts

Any administration despairs of a tax increase just before an election or a tax cut just after an election.

How About Spinach?

If we judged everything by appearances, nobody would eat an oyster!

Not Confused

A man never gets so confused in his thinking that he can't see the other fellow's duty.

Think About It

You may sometimes hear a dull sermon on Sunday, but you aren't out getting a flat tire going seventy-five miles an hour.

—Herbert V. Prochnow

The Pedestrian's Luck

Every man has his day, and the pedestrian gets his in an ambulance.

How to Win Friends

The way to win friends and influence people is to give others your candied opinion.

Not Necessarily

'Tis sweet to court, but, oh! how bitter, to court a gal, and then not git her!

Good Suggestion

Sometimes it is better to put off until tomorrow what you are likely to botch today.

Surprised

Behind every successful man stands a surprised mother-in-law.

Efficient

The only person ever to get his work done by Friday was Robinson Crusoe.

Only One Thing Left

After paying for the wedding, about the only thing a father has left to give away is the bride.

Punctuality

Punctuality is the art of guessing how late the other guy will be.

Vacation

Two weeks off is too often followed by two off weeks.

It Can't Be Done

He travels faster who has the ability to fold road maps.

Only One Worry

Historians tell us about the past and economics about the future. Only the present is confusing.

Lost in Thought

Too often the person who gets lost in thought does so because it's unfamiliar territory.

Following Our Example

Children are creatures who disgrace you by exhibiting in public the example you set for them at home.

Not Always Cheap

When you get a chance to buy things for a song, it's a good idea to check the accompaniment.

Good Question

If, as psychologists tell us, there is no such thing as pain, what is it some people give us?

They Learn the Tricks

Some persons are so busy learning the tricks of the trade that they never learn the trade.

It Isn't Easy Here Either

Some think that the moon won't be able to support life. Well, it's not such an easy thing on this old planet either.

A Bad Mistake

Then there was the bell ringer who got tangled in the rope and tolled himself off.

One Advantage

Slang has this advantage over pure English: when you use it, most people understand exactly what you mean.

The Right Place

Sign in optometrist's window: "If you don't see what you want, you've come to the right place."

Happens to Everyone

It used to be that a fool and his money were soon parted, but now it happens to everybody.

Can't Keep Quiet

An egotist is usually me-deep in conversation.

Hard Job

The head of a leading university says he is trying to develop a school the football team can be proud of.

It Helps

If at first you don't succeed, try looking in the wastebasket for the directions.

Handicap

It's tough on a woman who wants to make a success in business; she doesn't have a wife to advise her.

Don't Hesitate

He who hesitates misses the green light, gets bumped in the rear, and loses his parking place.   —*Herbert V. Prochnow*

It Doesn't Pay

Counterfeiting doesn't seem as prevalent as it once was, but with $1 worth less than 59 cents, it doesn't pay as well.

Hard to Realize

It's a terrible shock for most of us to find out that you can't economize without spending less money.

Always Busy

The average American works 120 days for the tax collector and the other 244 days for the installment collector.
                    —*Herbert V. Prochnow*

Don't Worry

If you fool some of the people all of the time, and all of the people some of the time, you need not worry; someone else will fool them the rest of the time.

Distributing Wealth

Nothing redistributes wealth like taxation and a big family.
                    —*Herbert V. Prochnow*

The Real Problem

All of us are more or less stupid occasionally, but it wouldn't be so bad if we didn't try to prove it.   *—Herbert V. Prochnow*

Why Governments Change

No leftist party stays in power long in any country because it must get out occasionally to let the conservatives pay the debts.

No Change

Adam fell for an apple, but millions of men have fallen for applesauce.

Wisdom

No one becomes wise who is sure he already is.

Too Big to Study

Whenever a person gets too big to study, he is as big as he will ever be.   *—Herbert V. Prochnow*

Very Considerate

You must say the Russians are considerate. Any trouble they start is started in other countries.

They Deserve It

There should be a special express lane into Heaven for school bus drivers and Little League umpires.

Can't Recall

Have you ever seen a jogger smile?

Changing Times

Old-timer: One who remembers when the moon inspired only romance instead of space travel.

At the Fountain of Knowledge

Some students drink deeply at the fountain of knowledge—others only gargle.

Hard to Educate

Some drivers show less improvement each year than the automobiles they drive. —*Herbert V. Prochnow*

It Could Be Worse

Things might be worse. Suppose your errors were published every day like those of a baseball player.

Listen

There is only one rule for being a good talker: learn to listen.

What It Shows

Early to bed and early to rise is a sure sign that you don't care for television.

Forget It

Don't worry if you start losing your memory. Just forget about it.

Willing

Everybody is willing to forget the past if it catches up with them.

It Isn't Easy

The goal of some ambitious people is not to be somebody, but to do somebody.

Naturally

Sign in a store: We buy old furniture. We sell antiques.

Just Wait for Them

Never try to keep up with the Joneses. Just wait and meet them on the way coming back.   —*Herbert V. Prochnow, Jr.*

Times Don't Change

Times haven't changed much because centuries ago Greek maidens in love used to sit and listen to a lyre all evening too.   —*Herbert V. Prochnow*

Pride

The less a person has, even brains, the prouder he is of it.
—*Herbert V. Prochnow*

A Helping Hand

Somebody is always ready to lend a helping hand if you have any trouble opening your billfold.

Laborsaving

One of the greatest laborsaving devices of today is tomorrow.

Inside Information

Never argue with your doctor; he has inside information.

Don't Go Too Far

It's smart to pick your friends, but not to pieces.

Elections

Some elections don't prove the people aren't conservative. They only prove that they don't get mad when they're prosperous.

Hard Lesson

The greatest boon to this generation financially was learning to spend the income of the next generation.

Gossip

For gossip to succeed, it has to be unreasonable enough to shock everyone and reasonable enough that a few will believe it.

Help the Country

Now is the time for all good men to come to the aid of both parties.

Often Necessary

Sometimes you've got to call a spade a spade to get it back from a neighbor.

One Advantage

One of the nicest features about old age is that you can whistle while you brush your teeth.

Simple

This fishing business is simple—all you have to do is get there yesterday when fish were biting.

Our Worry

What's worrying us is that the government is living not only beyond its own income but also beyond ours.

How to Lose Money

A sure way to lose money is to bet on a sure thing.

That's Different

When you have to swallow your own medicine, the spoon seems very large.

Exercise

The only exercise some people get is jumping to conclusions, running down friends, sidestepping responsibility, and pushing their luck.

Changes Your View

Nothing makes you more tolerant of a neighbor's noisy party than being there.

Service

Sign in pawnship window: See us at your earliest inconvenience.

Correct

News misprint: The motorist approached the coroner at ninety miles per hour.

Comfortably Unhappy

Money may not buy happiness, but with it you can be unhappy in perfect comfort.

Easier

It is much easier to be critical than correct.

To Be at Ease

To make yourself at ease, always underrate others.
—Herbert V. Prochnow, Jr.

The Computer

The computer is a moron. *—Peter Drucker*

It Took Practice

A person who is a good liar got that way by long practice.
—Herbert V. Prochnow

It's Wise to Jump

He is the kind of person who makes others jump—a reckless driver. *—Herbert V. Prochnow*

They Don't Need To

Money talks, but the folks who know how to save it don't.
—Herbert V. Prochnow, Jr.

Or Get a Different House

People who live in glass houses might as well answer the doorbell.

Might Help

All the world needs is an agreement not to have any more wars until the old ones are paid for.

What Was So Bad

When we look at the surplus of cotton, we wonder what was so bad about the boll weevil.

Lazy Not Wise

Early to bed and late to rise makes one lazy rather than wise.

Not Exciting

One way to avoid excitement is to live within your income.

Is That Fair?

Some persons insist that a fishing pole is a stick with a worm on both ends of it.

Too Fidgety

Many a fellow gets a reputation for being energetic when in truth he is merely fidgety.

Getting Attention

The quickest way to get undivided attention is to make a mistake.

Helping Fix Things

For fixing things around the house, nothing beats a checkbook.

A Real Executive

A real executive is one who trains others to handle his responsibilities.

Be Thrifty Anyway

Be thrifty when you're young, and when you're old you'll be able to afford the things that only the young can enjoy.

Make Others Happy

Never miss an opportunity to make others happy, even if you have to leave them alone to do it.

One Advantage

There is one thing that can be said about ignorance: it causes a lot of interesting arguments.

One Test

You are getting old if it takes you longer to rest than it did to get tired.

Always Risks

Progress always involves risks. You can't steal second base and keep your foot on first.

High Face Value

A smile can add a great deal to one's face value.

A Common Problem

How to stay in the groove without making it a rut is the problem of every executive.

You Have to Hurry

If you think twice before you speak, you'll never get into the conversation.

A Prescription

"What this country needs," said a prominent medical man, "is tranquility without tranquilizers."

Vocation and Vacation

Until a person takes as eager an interest in his vocation as in his vacation, he is not worth very much.

Could Talk Forever

Though I'm anything but clever, I could talk like that forever.
—*W. S. Gilbert*

Can't Understand

I have never been able to understand why it is that just because I am unintelligible nobody understands me.   —*Milton Mayer*

Not Strange

The average man seems able to detect a rattle in his car more quickly than one in his head.

One Good Point

A conceited person has at least one good point: He doesn't talk about other people.

Even a Small One

Most arguments about new cars start from scratch.

Is This Too Sensible?

Maybe the way to solve the farm problem is to consult the hardest hands instead of the best minds.

Making Friends

If your neighbor does you harm, show your desire to be a friend by buying one of his children a drum.

—*Herbert V. Prochnow*

Increasing Enthusiasm

Nothing increases your enthusiasm like having your own way. —*Herbert V. Prochnow, Jr.*

Too True

A man begins cutting his wisdom teeth the first time he bites off more than he can chew.

A Compact Car

For bringing a family closer together, there's nothing like a compact car.

Three Kinds of People

There are three kinds of people: The few who make things happen, the many who watch things happen, and those who have no idea what has happened.

A Right to His Opinion

Always be tolerant of a person who disagrees with you. After all, he has a right to his ridiculous opinion.

Keep Smiling

Keep smiling. It makes everyone wonder what you've been up to.

Playing It Safe

People don't always believe everything they hear, but often they repeat it just to be on the safe side.

Hard to Believe

Isn't it hard to believe that this nation was founded partly to avoid taxes?

Puzzling Words

Among the English language's many puzzling words is "economy," which means the large size in soap flakes and the small size in autos.

What It Indicates

A chip on the shoulder indicates that there's wood higher up.

One Thing He Needs

For the man who has everything: a calendar to remind him when the payments are due.

It Helps

More doors are opened with "please" than with keys.

Enjoy Your Garden

To enjoy your garden work, put on a wide hat and gloves, hold a trowel in one hand, and tell the man where to dig.

One Advantage

Laugh at "puppy love" if you like, but it's the only thing that can reconcile a boy to washing his neck and ears.

She Probably Did

The man who boasts he never made a mistake in his life may have a wife who did.

Is That Clear?

Be obscure clearly.   —*E. B. White*

Gets Worse

Work may not be as hard as it used to be, but it is certainly more taxing.

Works Both Ways

The driver is safer when the roads are dry; the roads are safer when the driver is dry.

Helpful

Another nice thing about a one-way street is that you can get bumped only in the rear.

No Influence

If you think you have influence, just try ordering somebody else's dog around.

A Wrong Number?

Uneasy lies the head that ignores a telephone call at night.

Easier

It's far easier to forgive an enemy after you've got even with him. —*Olin Miller*

It Isn't Enough

A liar needs a good memory. —*Quintilian*

Besides Money

Money isn't everything. After all, there are checks, charge accounts, and credit cards.

Unusual Problem

The dear old lady expressed the spirit of the day, whether intentionally or unintentionally, when she said that she could get along very well without the necessities of life, but she just couldn't be reconciled to getting along without the luxuries.

Our Sister States

It is said that the sister states are Miss Ouri, Mary Land, Allie Bama, Ida Ho, Callie Fornia, Della Ware, Louisa Ana, Minnie Sota, and Flora Da.

At No Time

Nobody can't never get nothing for nothing nowhere, no time, nohow.

Solved Hard Problem

It is reported that a young student recently stayed up all night figuring out what became of the sun when it went down. It finally dawned on him.

Lucky

Confucius say: "Man in barrel is lucky—to still have barrel."

Helpful

The trouble is that one extravagance always suggests another.

Never Successful

The scrupulously truthful man is never as great a success as a fisherman.

We Agree

Most people think they would rather be miserably rich than happily poor.

Improves with Time

Your temper is one of the few things that improves the longer you keep it.

Gratitude

Says the habitual borrower: "Lend me $10 and I'll be everlastingly indebted to you."

Not So Much

Some people take too much of vitamin "I."

At Least It's Done

After you decide nothing can be done, someone comes along and does it.

Same Objective

Many of us live expensively to impress our friends who live expensively to impress us.

Almost Succeeded

He planned to go on a vacation and forget everything. The first time he opened his suitcase, he discovered how nearly he had succeeded.

A Really Big One

Oh, give me grace to catch a fish, so large that even I, in talking about it afterward, may never need to lie!

Advice to Lawyers

If you have the law on your side, address the court; if you have the facts on your side, address the jury; but if you have neither the law nor the facts, abuse the other side.

How to Get Ahead

Some people would get along better financially by spending less money than they haven't earned, for things they don't need, to impress people they don't like.

Occasionally

The person who does a lot of talking is bound to be right—some time.

The Problem

We like the man whose impulse is to say "yes" much better than the one whose impulse it is to say "no," but the trouble is that the former never seems to have anything to lend.

Not Easy

Few of us can stand prosperity. Another man's I mean.

—Mark Twain

Learning by Doing

If we learn by doing things, a lot of people are going to keep on being ignorant.   *—Herbert V. Prochnow*

Not Necessarily Safe

The American home has been put on a sound basis with radio and television.

What They Discover

When a man and woman marry they become one, and then they discover which one.

That's Our Experience

Shake and shake the catsup bottle, none will come, and then a lot'll.   *—Richard Armour*

Absentminded

And there was the absentminded motorist who changed his oil every day and his shirt every 2,000 miles.

Thankful

Perhaps we ought to be thankful to the follow who keeps us so busy listening to his troubles that we haven't time to think of our own.

She Ain't Benzine

Mary had a little lamp, she filled it with benzine; she went to light her little lamp, and hasn't since benzine.

They Fall in the Fall

The autumn leaves are falling, are falling here and there. They're falling through the atmosphere, and also through the air.

Just So

The rain, it falleth on the just, and also on the unjust fellow; but chiefly on the just, because the unjust steals the just's umbrella.

More Expensive Too

We have discovered that family ties are stronger at Christmas-time—and louder, too.

Advertising

Sign on a bakery truck: What Foods These Morsels Be.

Too Bad

The church bell is far more important than the fire bell, but it does not make the people run nearly so fast.

Criticism

Criticism is one of the few things people would rather give than take.

Usually

Those rainy days, for which a man saves, usually come during his vacation.

Or Athlete's Salary

Movie actor's salary: The haul of fame.   —*The Cab Stand*

No Use Trying

Dignity is a thing that can't be preserved in alcohol.

Fish Story

Confucius say: "No man who catches large fish goes home through alley."   —*Herbert V. Prochnow*

Wise Decision

A teenager always reaches for a chair when she answers the telephone.

Leaves No Impression

A shallow thinker seldom makes a deep impression.

Most Annoying

The most annoying thing about a stand-patter is not his stand but his patter.

Grandson Agrees

The man who never thought anything of walking ten miles a day now has a grandson who doesn't think so much of it either.

Laughable Argument

If both sides of an argument make you laugh, you are either stupid or broad-minded.   —*Herbert V. Prochnow*

Serving Self Only

Too many of us conduct our lives on the cafeteria plan: self-service only.

Plenty of Shortening

The recipe for successful after-dinner speaking includes using plenty of shortening.

An Opportunist

An opportunist is one who meets the wolf at the door and appears the next day in a fur coat.

One Advantage

The wonderful thing about a dull party is that you can get home early.   —*Herbert V. Prochnow*

Economics Lesson

The reason talk is cheap is that the supply always exceeds the demand.   —*Herbert V. Prochnow*

Inflation

Money may still talk, but every year it makes less cents.

Helpful

It is always easier to arrive at a firm conviction about a problem after you know what the boss thinks.

That's Different

The man who said that every knock is a boost never drove an old car.

A Jefferson Invention

Thomas Jefferson invented the swivel chair, which showed how well he knew bureaucrats.　*—Herbert V. Prochnow*

Unusual Inventions

An alarm clock with half a bell on it, so when two people are rooming together, it just wakes one of them.

Carnations with buttonholes already attached to them.

Red, green, yellow, and blue sleeping tablets which you take before retiring so you'll dream in technicolor.

A stepladder without steps in it, for washing windows in the cellar.　*—Colonel Lemuel Q. Stoopnagle*

Or Vice Versa

Leisure time is when your wife can't find you.

Keeping It Working

Even when a marriage is made in heaven, the maintenance work has to be done on earth.

An Idea

Someone should invent a car with brakes that will get tight when the driver does!

Night Driving

The increase in automobile accidents late at night is due to a combination of head lights and light heads.

—Herbert V. Prochnow

An Uplifter

One of the world's greatest uplifters is the alarm clock.

Putters Around

The average golfer is just a fellow who putters around.

And Succeeding

Another thing that seems to be wrong with the world is that one-half the people are trying to fool the other half.

Doctor's Instructions

If you're thin, the doctor says, "Don't eat fast." If you're fat, he says, "Don't eat. Fast."   —*Herbert V. Prochnow*

A Joy to All

His thoughts were slow, his words were few and never formed to glisten, but he was a joy to all his friends—because he knew how to listen.

It Doesn't Help

The only people who listen to both sides of an argument are the next-door neighbors.

You Said It

There are bigger things in life than money: bills.

Sometimes Shorter

The average time between throwing something out and needing it again is about two weeks.

Sales Promotion

Sign seen in a service station: Courteous and efficient self-service.

Keep Smiling

Smile and the world smiles with you; kick, and you kick alone; for the cheering grin will let you in where the kicker is unknown.

A Struggle

Life is a struggle to keep earning capacity to yearning capacity.

Human Error

To err is only human, but when you wear out the eraser before you've used up the pencil, you're overdoing it.

It Helps

Nature couldn't make us perfect, so she did the next best thing—she made us blind to our faults.

It Doesn't Take Long

A fool and his money are soon invited places.

Hard to Explain

If you don't believe in luck, how else do you explain the success of those you don't like?

The Key

The key to success, according to today's youth, is the one that fits the ignition.

A Kind Old Lady

Said the kind old lady to the Internal Revenue clerk, "I do hope you'll give my money to some nice country."

Full Value

He who drops a quarter in the contribution plate generally expects a $50 sermon.

In a Fog

People, like boats, toot loudest when they are in a fog.

Think About This

Don't finish anything you aren't able to start.

Upsetting

Nothing is so upsetting to a person as to have company drop in to see the house looking like it usually does.

Before and After Sixteen

Up to sixteen a lad is a boy scout; after that, he is a girl scout.

Hard to Know

Men and melons are hard to know.   *—Benjamin Franklin*

Bureaucracy

There is very little to admire in bureaucracy, but you have got to hand it to the Internal Revenue Service.

—James L. Rogers

Truth in Advertising

A plaque on the wall of a psychiatrist's office: No one in his right mind ever comes to see me.

This Is Fame

An architect designed a building so beautiful other architects admired it.

Line Is Often Busy

The line is too often busy when conscience wishes to speak.

Not Common

Common sense is uncommon.

Gossip

Gossip goes in both ears and comes out of the mouth greatly enlarged.

Plagiarism

A plagiarist is a person who improves on something that was poorly written. —*Herbert V. Prochnow, Jr.*

Nash Nuances

I would live all my life in nonchalance and insouciance were it not for making a living, which is rather a nouciance.

—*Ogden Nash*

American Families

The thing that impresses me most about America is the way parents obey their children.

—*Edward, Duke of Windsor, 1957*

Pedestrians

A zombie has no mind of his own and walks around without knowing where he's going or what he's doing. . . . In Hollywood they call them "pedestrians." —*Bob Hope*

Education

When a subject becomes totally obsolete we make it a required course. —*Peter Drucker*

Infancy

Infancy is the period of our lives when, according to Wordsworth, "Heaven lies about us." The world begins lying about us pretty soon afterward. —*Ambrose Bierce*

Similes Can Be Humorous and Wise

No more social position than an onion. —*Cliff Edwards*

A night as cold and damp as a dog's nose. —*Fulton Oursler*

Frivolous as meringue. —*W. S. Ethridge*

Useless as a pulled tooth. —*Mary Roberts Rinehart*

Mysterious as chop suey. —*A. L. Hottes*

In her single person she managed to produce the effect of a majority. —*Ellen Glasgow*

No more sense of direction than a bunch of firecrackers.
—*Rob Wagner*

Use Metaphors in Speech and Conversation

He nudged me with a wink. —*Corey Ford*

He strains his conversation through a cigar.
—*Hamilton Mabie*

She's the plot of his life's story. —*Lewis Orvis Hervey*

She shifted her face into neutral.   —*Unknown*

The general creased a little in the middle to signify he was bowing.   —*Negley Farson*

Streets mushroomed with umbrellas.   —*Maxine McBride*

I buttoned up the pockets of my sympathy.

—*Somerset Maugham*

They Never Die

Old college deans never die—they only lose their faculties.

Old politicians never die—they just run once too often.

Old golfers never die—they just putter away.

Old gardeners never die—they just spade away.

Old volcanoes never die—they just blow their tops.

Old quarterbacks never die—they just pass away.

Old cows never die—they just kick the bucket.

Old farmers never die—they just go to seed.

Old mufflers never die—they just get exhausted.

Old bankers never die—they just lose interest.

—*Herbert V. Prochnow*

Chapter 4

DID YOU KNOW THESE FACTS?

Latin America's Growth

By the year 2000, Latin America's teeming millions may be exceeded only by those of Asia. If the present growth trend continues to the end of the century, Latin America will have almost twice as many people as the United States and Canada.

Alphabets of Various Nations

The alphabets of different languages contain the following number of letters: English, 26; French, 23; Italian, 20; Spanish, 27; German, 26; Slavonic, 27; Russian, 41; Latin, 22; Greek, 24; Hebrew, 22; Arabic, 28; Persian, 32; Turkish, 33; Sanskrit, 50.

Pity the poor Chinese! To read intelligently, they must learn at least 3,000 characters. And that isn't all! Wise Chinese must know at least 40,000 characters.

Sold for Just $400!

The name of Walter Hunt, inventor of the safety pin, is little known. In 1849, ten years before he died, Hunt began fiddling with a little piece of wire, developed a safety pin, and finally sold the idea for just $400, which is all he ever made from the invention.

It Must Be Those Vitamins

In 1776, only 1 American out of 50 (2 percent) was 65 or older. By 1900, 1 out of every 25 (4 percent) was over 65. In 1980, 1 out of every 9 Americans (11 percent) was 65 or older.

How Long Animals Live

Wonder how birds and animals would look on birthdays if they knew when theirs came around! Of all the birds, swans have the most birthdays; they have been known to live 300 years.

Among animals, whales are entitled to the most birthday candles. Their average life is about 1,000 years. The whales that follow the ships in the Atlantic Ocean today also followed the little ships in Columbus's small fleet back in 1492.

Elephants, under good conditions, will live 400 years.

Tortoises have many birthdays too. They live considerably past 100 years.

The average number of birthdays of horses is 25 to 30; of hogs, bears, and wolves, 20. Of the smaller animals, dogs and cats usually have 10 to 15 birthdays, and squirrels and rabbits 7 or 8.

The Good Old Days

Early automobile buyers found it hard to resist this advertisement of the Buffalo (New York) Electric Carriage Co.: "Most automobiles look ungainly and unsightly. The Buffalo Stanhope is an exception. It is built on ordinary carriage lines, has wood wheels, hard rubber tires, ball bearings throughout. Will seat three persons. Storage battery has capacity for a 50-mile run. Battery can be fully recharged in three hours. Price, $1,800."

History of the Flag

The first flag of the United States was the Grand or Great Union Flag, which was raised on Prospect Hill in Somerville, Massachusetts, by George Washington's Continental soldiers on New Year's Day in 1776. The following year, Congress created our flag, which has thirteen stars and thirteen stripes, representing the thirteen colonies. When Francis Scott Key saw the flag waving triumphantly over Fort McHenry in 1814 and was inspired to write "The Star-Spangled Banner," it had fifteen stars and fifteen stripes. More stars and more stripes were added for each new state until 1820, when Congress decided that the national flag would have thirteen stripes, and a new star would be added with the admission of each new state.

How It Started

James Watt, the Scottish inventor who built the first steam engine, also named its energy—horsepower. This term was necessary. There was no other way for people to understand or measure the power of the steam engine. So, Watt, with a mature horse, rope, and pulleys, determined how much weight the horse could lift in a minute—a 3,300-pound weight to a height of 10 feet in one minute.

Then Watt discovered that his steam engine could lift a 3,300-pound weight to a height of 100 feet. Thus, the steam engine provided ten times as much power as one mature horse. Watt termed his machine a 10-horsepower engine. And horsepower is still the measurement for gasoline engines, diesel engines, electric motors and even atomic reactors.

—Good Reading

Facts That May Surprise You

Here are a few items from historical records that may surprise you:

In the early days of the United States, onions were hung over doors in the belief that they would counteract diseases that visitors might bring in.

President William Henry Harrison, with a basket on his arm, did his own shopping for the White House.

It took seventy-six years for the Great Pyramid of Egypt to be built.

Robinson Crusoe's real name was Alexander Selkirk.

The initial S in former President Harry S Truman's name does not stand for a name; it is merely an alphabetical addition.

You Win and Lose

The great baseball pro, Cy Young, holds the all-time record for winning the most games—511 wins—during his career from 1890 to 1911. He pitched in 906 games, completed 751 of them, and once pitched 23 consecutive hitless innings. He also held the record for having lost more games than any other big league pitcher: 313.

Almost Speechless

There are more than 400,000 words in the English language; the average person knows or can use less than 3 percent of them. Even journalists are able to use only about 20,000 words, only 5 percent of the total number.

It's Hard to Believe These Facts

The Pacific end of the Panama Canal is farther east than the Atlantic end.

Venice, Italy, and Montreal, Canada, are in about the same latitude.

The entire continent of South America lies farther east than Florida.

Cuba would reach from New York to Chicago.

Texas is as large as 212 Rhode Islands.

The American Flag

The Congressional resolution determining the design of our flag was adopted June 14, 1777.

The Stars and Stripes may claim antiquity among national flags. Here are the dates on which various national flags were established: Great Britain, 1801; France, 1794; Spain, 1785; Italy, 1848.

The flag was first carried around the world on the ship *Columbia,* sailing from Boston, September 30, 1787, and returning August 10, 1790.   —*The Royal Neighbor*

Steam Is Best

The year was 1902, and the "Locomobile" motor car was advertised by the Locomobile Company of America, 7 East 42nd Street, New York City, with this assurance: "Steam is the Best Motive Power for Automobiles." It was offered with or without a Victoria top.

Texas

The town of Texline, Texas, is nearer to the state capitals of Colorado, Kansas, New Mexico, Oklahoma, and Wyoming than it is to its own state capital, Austin. The sun in its journey around the earth shines longer on Texas than on any other state.

It Wasn't Easy Either

Tennis was originally played without racquets. Players hit the ball over the net with the palms of their hands.

The First Football

The first football match between U.S. colleges—Harvard and Yale—was played in 1876.

There Is Hope for Everyone

The garlic plant belongs to the lily family.

Is That Clear?

A Louisiana attorney, hired by a New York firm to trace the abstract of a deed, went back to 1803, the year Louisiana was purchased from France. Then the firm wrote the lawyer that he would have to trace the ownership of the land further back than that. In due time he did so, reporting by letter as follows:

"Dear Sirs: I traced your deed back to 1803. Here it is complete. As you probably know, Louisiana was purchased from France in 1803; France had acquired Louisiana from the Spanish as the result of a successful war against the Spaniards. The Spaniards acquired Louisiana as the result of the explorations of an Italian named Columbus. Columbus was financially backed by Isabella and Ferdinand of Spain. They were given permission for Columbus's expedition by the Pope. The Pope is the vicar of Christ. Christ is the Son of God. God made Louisiana!"

Biblical Data

Old Testament prophecy was perhaps the highest product of the Hebrew religion.

The word "psalm" comes from a Greek word meaning "a song accompanied by string instruments."

The prayer of Jesus on the cross, "Father, into thy hands I commend my spirit" (a quotation from Psalm 31:5), is the first prayer many have learned.

The 23 miles from Jericho to Jerusalem is an uphill journey of some 4,000 feet.

There are 280 verses in the New Testament bearing on the subject of the Resurrection.

Micah predicted details of the birth of Jesus 700 years before it happened.   —*The War Cry,* New York

How Prophetic!

In 1894, when there were only four automobiles in the United States, a New York publisher brought out the first issue of the *Horseless Age,* a trade magazine, which contained this prophetic statement:

"... Those who have taken the pains to search beneath the surface for the great tendencies of the age see what a giant industry is struggling into being."

Four years later, in 1898, a Massachusetts manufacturer made the unprecedented announcement that 50 automobiles had been produced and sold in a 12-month period. In quick succession, a "stable" for renting, selling, storing, and repairing motor vehicles was opened in Boston; an automotive show was held in Manhattan; and a firm to buy and sell used motor cars was established there also that year.   —*Sunshine Magazine*

A Major Decision

It was in 1867 that William Seward, then secretary of state, persuaded a reluctant Congress to ratify the treaty with Russia that made Alaska a possession of the United States. The purchase price of $7,200,000 was considered exorbitant even though it worked out to about $12 per square mile, or less than 2 cents an acre. On discovery of the gold fields in the 1880s, Seward's Folly was acknowledged as a masterpiece of foresightedness.

Times Have Changed

Fifty years ago folks boiled coffee and settled it with an egg; the only reds known were red flannels. A candidate had to be economy-minded to get elected to office; neighbors asked about your family and meant it; and when a man dressed for the evening, he put on his nightshirt. Folks used toothpicks and were still polite. Parents were the only baby-sitters. Rip Van Winkle slept twenty years and no one asked him to endorse a mattress.

If Any Creatures Are Looking

If there were creatures on Mars using telescopes to study the earth, the first evidence of life they would see is the Great Wall of China because it is the largest structure ever built on our globe. Made of bricks nearly 2,200 years ago, it is 1,500 miles long from Kiangsu to the sea, varies from 18 to 35 feet high, and is thick enough for a road on top. It cost the lives of an estimated 400,000 workers, many of whom were buried inside the wall, which has been called "the longest cemetery in the world."

Some Do Even More

According to one statistician, the average person spends at least thirteen years of his or her life talking. On a normal day, about 18,000 words are likely to be used—roughly the equivalent of a book of 54 pages. In the course of a single year, your words would fill 66 books, each book containing 800 pages.

Thanksgiving

Thanksgiving, a traditional American holiday, did not originate in America. About 3,000 years before it was observed here, God spoke to Moses in the days when the Israelites had just escaped from Egypt. They were having their first experience in the wilderness of the Sinai. The original proclamation from God is reported in Exodus 23:16: "Thou shalt keep the feast of harvest, the first fruits of thy labors, which thou has sown in the field: and the feast of in-gathering, which is in the end of the year, when thou hast gathered in thy labors out of the field."

It Was No Joke to Him

It was a joke that had been tried on every embryonic engineer since the electric light was hardly a gleam in Edison's brain. The novice engineer would be assigned the "impossible" task of frosting electric light bulbs on the inside.

A new engineer at General Electric, Marvin Pipkin, was

put through the usual routine. Not being aware that it was a joke, he discovered a way not only to frost bulbs on the inside, but also to etch the glass with soft, rounded pits which gave the bulbs added strength and effected a maximum diffusion of the light.

Fortunately, no "wise guy" told him that he had been assigned the impossible, so he went ahead and accomplished it! —*Executives' Digest*

Did You Know?

George Washington never lived in the city named for him, Washington, D.C.

The Only One

The only president of the United States to be married in the White House was Grover Cleveland.

Historical Knowledge

The first United States president to wear long trousers was Thomas Jefferson.

Lewis Carroll

A vivid illustration of the pseudonym is the authorship of two of the world's best known fantasies: *Alice in Wonderland* and *Through the Looking Glass.* Everybody knows, of course, that the author of these gems was "Lewis Carroll."

Or was it?

The fact is, there was no such person in literature as Lewis Carroll. This name is honored throughout the world, and the classic is said to have been quoted more than any other work, except the Bible and Shakespeare, and the original manuscript of *Alice in Wonderland* sold for 15,000 pounds seventy years later.

And yet, Lewis Carroll was none other than Charles Lutwidge Dodgson, a mathematician in England, who died in

1898 at the age of sixty-six. He was shy in the company of adults but loved children and told exciting stories to the children.

To the six-year-old Alice Liddell, Dodgson told his story of the Wonderland. Alice clapped her hands and exclaimed, "I never want to forget this best of all stories!" Dodgson put the story in writing, making Alice Liddell the heroine. Then he gave her the written story.

It Looked Large Then

When Edgar Allan Poe finally sold his famous poem "The Raven," he was paid $10 for it. Now the original manuscript is valued at $250,000.

One Match

One tree can make a million matches. One match can destroy a million trees.

Who Said It?

Here are common phrases used every day. See if you have any idea where they came from:

"Thanks for nothing."
"No limits but the sky."
"To give the devil his due."
"A peck of troubles."
"Let the worst come to the worst."
"A finger in every pie."
"Every dog has his day."
"A wild goose chase."

Give up? Every one of these phrases appeared in one book, *Don Quixote,* written more than 350 years ago by Miguel de Cervantes.

It Wasn't Easy Then

Jacob M. Murdock loaded his family into a Packard 30 seven-passenger, open touring car on April 12, 1908, and set out from

Pasadena, California, for New York City. His was the first family to make a cross-country trek by automobile. There were no paved roads, no service stations, no roadside restaurants, no motels, and no road maps. The trip took 32 days, 5½ hours, with Sundays off, to cover a total of 3,674 miles, much of it across open country.

They Make All the Picnics

In proportion to its size, the ant has the largest brain in the animal kingdom.

Young Geniuses

Thomas Jefferson wrote the Declaration of Independence when he was thirty-three.

Alexander Hamilton was a member of Congress at twenty-five and a member of George Washington's cabinet at thirty-two.

Daniel Webster entered Congress at thirty.

Henry Clay was appointed senator at twenty-nine, before he was of constitutional age.

Chaucer was well known at court as a poet when he was but twenty-five.

Livy began his *History of Rome* at the age of twenty-four.

Molière finished a comedy, his best, at seventeen.

Milton wrote "Comus," esteemed by some as one of his most charming poems, at twenty-six.

Keats made himself immortal in English literature before his death at twenty-four.

Beethoven was a skilled composer at nineteen.

Ford started his first car while in his thirties.

Edison invented the incandescent electric light when he was only thirty-two.

A "Vertical" River

The most vertical river in the world is the River Jordan, in the Middle East. In a little more than one hundred miles, it drops from 1,700 feet above sea level to 1,300 feet below. Nothing on this planet compares with the River Jordan.

From its source in the springs of Mount Hermon, it winds so much that its flowing distance is over 200 miles—more than twice the straight line. After about 35 miles, it has dropped from a height of 1,700 feet to sea level. Then for ten miles it plunges through cataracts and whirlpools, and pours into the Sea of Galilee nearly 700 feet below the level of the sea.

It rushes through the Sea of Galilee so rapidly that its waters do not mingle with the waters of Galilee, though the sea is fourteen miles long. Then it keeps tumbling and rushing through huge gorges for over a hundred miles toward the Dead Sea. There it reaches a low of 1,300 feet below sea level.

The land adjoining is the lowest land area in the world. Death Valley in California—the deepest in America—reaches only a level of 276 feet below the sea.

The salty Dead Sea into which the Jordan empties is in some places 1,300 feet deep. The bottom of the Dead Sea is the deepest natural hole in this earth, measuring about half a mile below the level of the sea.   —*Sunshine Magazine*

Exodus of 2 Million

Historians claim that Moses led more than 2 million people out of Egypt in that historic exodus.

Can You Solve It?

Ten weary travelers sought refuge in a wayside inn on a dark and stormy night.

"I have only nine rooms, no more," the landlord said. "Eight men can each have one room, but the ninth must serve for two."

Then the host devised a most ingenious plan:

In a room marked A, two men were placed; the third was lodged in B. The fourth to C was then assigned, the fifth retired in D. In E the sixth was tucked away, in F the seventh man; the eighth and ninth in G and H, and then to A he ran, wherein the host had put two travelers and taking one, the tenth and last, he lodged him safe in I.

Nine single rooms, a room for each, were made to serve for ten. And this is what puzzles me, and many wiser men.

In Old School Days

Times have changed. If you don't believe it, read the following rules that were in force at the famous Mt. Holyoke College in the year 1837:

"No young lady shall become a member of Mt. Holyoke Seminary who cannot kindle a fire, mash potatoes, and repeat the multiplication table and at least two-thirds of the shorter catechism.

"Every member of the school shall walk a mile a day unless a freshet, earthquake, or some other calamity prevent.

"No young lady shall devote more than an hour a day to miscellaneous reading.

"No young lady is expected to have gentlemen acquaintances unless they are returned missionaries or agents of benevolent societies." —*Epworth Herald*

The Mysteries of Nature

The speed of monarch butterflies has been recorded at about ten miles per hour when they are cruising, but they can sprint as fast as thirty miles per hour. One tagged butterfly was captured, released, and captured again, recording a flight of 80 miles in one day. The longest recorded flight of a monarch was 1,870 miles from Toronto, Canada, to San Luis Potosi, Mexico.

The monarch usually lives about only nine months or less. How can a monarch butterfly then find its way to the remote areas it flies only once?

The Result

The average intake of calories is 3,000 per day per person in the United States—leaving up to half the population overweight.

Chapter 5

Stories and Comments from Unusual Lives

Government Worthy of Trust

We scorn panaceas. We respect the fortitude, the courage, the staying power of the American people. We show that respect by always speaking the plain truth, as we know it.

And we are confident for precisely this same reason: We believe in the people. We believe in the ingenuity and the industry of the American as resources that no nation on earth can match. We believe in his capacity to work, to save, to invent, to sacrifice, to create, to dream good dreams—and to bring them to true life.

To do all these things, the people need but one thing: a government they can trust—a government worthy of that trust.

—George M. Humphrey

Hardship

Alexander Pope, the famous English poet (1688–1744), who was the first English writer to make money from his work, was only 4 feet 6 inches tall, suffered from poor health most of his life, and was so frail that he wore a corset to stand upright. His poetry was very popular and is still widely quoted.

Stay in College

World-famous prizefighter Muhammad Ali was once asked by a young man what he should do with his life. The heavyweight's reply was, "Stay in college, get the knowledge. And stay there until you're through. If they can make penicillin out of moldy bread, they can sure make something out of you!"

Unusual Achievement

At Exeter, New Hampshire, a youth was asked to address his schoolmates, but each attempt that he made was a fiasco. Here in his own bitter words is his confession: "I could not speak before the school. Many a piece did I commit to memory, and recite and rehearse in my own room, over and over again, and yet, when the day came, when my name was called, and all eyes turned to my seat, I could not raise myself from it. When the occasion was over, I went home and wept bitter tears of mortification." Later the youth determined that he would conquer his timidity, if he died in the attempt. That he succeeded admirably is indicated in the mere fact of his identity. He was Daniel Webster, often still acclaimed as the greatest orator America has ever produced.   —*Journal of Living*

Being Wholly Alive

I wouldn't swap one wrinkle of my face for all the elixirs of youth. All of these wrinkles represent a smile, a grimace of pain and disappointment ... some part of being fully alive.   ·
—*Helen Hayes*

America

The meaning of our word America flows from one pure source. Within the soul of America is the freedom of mind and spirit in man. Here alone are the open windows through which pours the sunlight of the human spirit. Here alone, human dignity is not a dream but a major accomplishment.   —*Herbert Hoover*

Confidence in the Value of Money

Confidence in the value of money is one of the greatest spurs to economic progress, because it is an incentive to save, and it is our people's savings over the years—large and small savings alike—which have built up our country.

—*George M. Humphrey*

Why a Twenty-One-Gun Salute?

One signer of the Declaration of Independence, Francis Hopkinson of New Jersey, was a notorious doodler. After his death, a story was written about his doodling. Hopkinson, late in 1776, was toying with the year "1776," a famous one in American history. He finally came up with the idea of adding the figures across and found that they totaled twenty-one. He then said to himself, "Why not a twenty-one-gun salute for the presidents?" He submitted his idea to members of Congress, who liked and approved it. It has been in use ever since.

Not Too Bad

Many years ago, an Englishwoman, perhaps a bit envious, told James McNeill Whistler that she thought the politeness of the French was all on the surface. The artist replied: "That is a very good place for it to be."

Sad If True

Historian Arnold Toynbee said: "Of the twenty-two civilizations that appear in history, nineteen of them collapsed when they reached the moral state the United States is in now."

Prayer for America

Almighty God, we make our earnest prayer that Thou keep the United States in Thy holy protection; that Thou wilt incline the hearts of the citizens to cultivate a spirit of subordination and obedience to government; to entertain a brotherly affection and love for one another and for their fellow citizens of the United States at large. And finally, that Thou wilt most graciously be pleased to dispose of us all to do justice, to love mercy, and to demean ourselves with that charity, humility and pacific temper of mind which were the characteristics of the divine Author of our blessed religion, and without a humble imitation of whose example in these things we can never hope to be a happy nation.

Grant our supplications we beseech Thee, through Jesus Christ, our Lord. Amen.   *—George Washington*

The Time Will Come

Once the great Lord Melbourne, then prime minister of England, asked a young man named Disraeli what he would like to be. Disraeli boldly replied, "prime minister of England." Few men in world history present a more remarkable illustration of the ability to overcome hardship than Disraeli. Without opportunity, he struggled through the middle classes and the upper groups of his country. Three times he was defeated in parliamentary elections. When he made his first speech in the House of Commons, he was ridiculed, hissed, and jeered. He cried out, "The time will come when you will hear me." And the time did come. He was determined. With courage and confidence he fought his way from the back benches of the House of Commons to leadership as prime minister of the British Empire.   *—Herbert V. Prochnow*

A Businessman's Philosophy

Entrepreneur/merchant Marshall Field once said, "Each and every man ought to interest himself in public affairs. There's no happiness in mere dollars. After they are acquired, one can use but a very moderate amount. It is given a man to eat so much, to wear so much, and to have so much shelter, and more he cannot use. When money has supplied these, its mission, so far as the individual is concerned, is fulfilled, and a man must look still further and higher. It is only in wide public affairs, where money is a moving force toward the general welfare, that the possessor of it can possibly find pleasure and that only in constantly doing more. The greatest good a man can do is to cultivate himself, develop his talents and powers in order that he may be of greater service to humanity."

Something for Everybody

Like other presidents, Abraham Lincoln suffered from the importunities of job seekers and persons looking for special favors, which once drove him to ask Surgeon General Barnes where he could get the smallpox. "Then," he said, "I shall have something I can give to everybody."

The Same Courage and Common Sense

If we as Americans show the same courage and common sense that motivated the men who sat at Philadelphia and gave us the Declaration of Independence, and later the Constitution of the U.S., there is no domestic problem we cannot solve, and no foreign foe we need ever fear.   —*William F. Knowland*

Leadership

But above all these matters, I venture to suggest that one challenge rises to tower over all others. We must provide the moral leadership, that steadfastness of spirit and mind, which alone can make us worthy of the high commission that history has conferred upon us.

We must care more for truth than success. We must care more for the hopes of the people than the votes of the people.

We must always worry more about our problems than the headlines. We must scorn the glib promise, the false phrase, the shallow excuse, and the clever evasion.

—*George M. Humphrey*

Be Humble

In our great pride at being the arsenal of democracy we must remember that we are also regarded as the arsenal of hope. Great leadership in such a righteous cause requires that a nation be humble—before its God and its fellowmen.
    —*Omar N. Bradley, former chairman, Joint Chiefs of Staff*

When We Pray

It is for us to pray not for tasks equal to our powers, but for powers equal to our tasks; to go forward with a great desire forever beating at the door of our hearts as we travel toward our distant goal.   —*Helen Keller*

History

Napoleon, so brilliant that countless books were written about him in the century after his death, was Waterlooed by the middle-aged son of an English musician, voted by his classmates at Eton as the "boy least likely to do anything."

How to Give Advice

I have found the best way to give advice to your children is to find out what they want and then advise them to do it.
    —*Harry S Truman*

Your Obligation

People owe this marvelous world whatever talents they can give it. They owe enough to the world to be a part of it, to use their talents to make others happy.   —*Mary Martin*

It Never Happened

When I look back on all these worries, I remember the story of the old man who said, on his death bed, that he had a lot of trouble in his life, most of which never happened.
    —*Winston Churchill*

A Beautiful Land

This is a beautiful land. But the foreigner might never know it if he judged only by our literature. A refugee said: "When I read your books I thought America was made up of nothing but slums, and factories, and smokestacks, and gasoline tanks, and miles and miles of trucks and dump heaps."

—*Paul Austin Wolfe*

Efficiency

Napoleon is reported to have had a rule that none of his incoming mail was to be opened for a period of three weeks, on the theory that most of the problems they raised would have solved themselves in that time.

In 1,000 Years

A thousand years hence, perhaps in less, America may be what Europe is now ... the noblest work of human wisdom, the grand scene of human glory, the fair cause of freedom that rose and fell.   —*Thomas Paine*

Forget It and Get Going

The world doesn't stop when you lose. I suffer over a loss like everyone else, but it's how soon you forget it and get going again that's important.

—*Tom Landry, former football coach of the Dallas Cowboys*

God in Every Person

I believe that God is in every person, and therefore, I don't get angry with people and I don't hate people. If something bad happens—I forget it right away, or at least ten minutes later.   —*George Burns*

Could This Happen?

I believe that the heaviest blow ever dealt at liberty's head will be dealt by this nation (the United States) in the ultimate failure of its example to the earth. —*Charles Dickens*

The First Principle

America is much more than a geographical fact. It is a political and moral fact—the first community in which men set out in principle to institutionalize freedom, responsible government, and human equality. —*Adlai Stevenson*

Real Fiction

Income tax returns are the most imaginative fiction being written today. —*Herman Wouk*

They Came Earlier

My folks didn't come over on the *Mayflower,* but they were here to meet the boat. —*Will Rogers*

What Turns Up

When you're down and out, something always turns up—and it's usually the noses of your friends. —*Orson Welles*

Those Who Dream

It may be those who do most, dream most. —*Stephen Leacock*

Disappointment

Anyone who expects something for nothing is all the better for being disappointed, because he learns something.
—*Henry Ford*

An Architect's Mistakes

A doctor can bury his mistakes but an architect can only advise his client to plant vines.   —*Frank Lloyd Wright*

Canada

Canada has never been a melting pot; more like a tossed salad.
—*Arnold Edinborough*

Humility

Don't be humble. You're not that great.   —*Golda Meir*

Learning About Yourself

You learn more about yourself campaigning for just one week than in six months with a psychoanalyst.
—*Adlai Stevenson II*

Still in Trouble

I am dying as I have lived—beyond my means.   —*Oscar Levant*

Your Library

Perhaps no place in any community is so democratic as the town library. The only entrance requirement is interest.
—*Mrs. Lyndon Baines Johnson*

Your Enemies

Forgive your enemies, but don't forget their names.
—*John F. Kennedy*

No Yes Men

I don't want any yes-men around me. I want everybody to tell me the truth even if it costs them their jobs.   —*Samuel Goldwyn*

Best for the Common Man

(America is) still the best country for the common man—white or black ... if he can't make it here he won't make it anywhere else. —*Eric Hoffer*

A Short Distance

History is the short trudge from Adam to atom.
                                        —*Leonard Louis Levinson*

Government Policy

Now, what is it we are trying to do? I think everybody in this country wants lower taxes. I am sure myself that we must have lower taxes in America if America is to be the land of opportunity for the young man. We want to keep it that way; we want to keep it the land of opportunity for the young man. That means we cannot take so much money by taxes from all the people in America and put that money into big government as we have been doing. We have to decrease that expenditure.
                                        —*George M. Humphrey*

His One Question

Edward W. Spencer was the first Northwestern University student life saver. At the wreck of the *Lady Elgin* off Winnetka, Illinois, on Lake Michigan, September 8, 1860, Spencer swam through the heavy surf sixteen times, rescuing seventeen persons in all. In the delirium of exhaustion which followed, his oft-repeated question was: "Did I do my best?"
                    —*From a bronze plaque on Patten Gymnasium,*
                        Northwestern University, Evanston, Illinois

Making the System Work

Much as it may be decried, the cold fact remains that ours is an economy actuated by profits. A certain return on money is necessary to make our system work. —*Bernard Baruch*

How to Honor Christmas

I will honor Christmas in my heart, and try to keep it all the year. —*Charles Dickens*

Financial Responsibility

Budgets, of course, are only estimates. When you are working with figures as large as government figures of income and expense, differences between estimates and actual performance can easily arise....

Balancing this budget is not simply a bookkeeping exercise or a businessman's fetish. It is the very keystone of financial responsibility. —*George M. Humphrey*

One Christmas

In the Austrian village of Hallein on Christmas Eve, in 1818, the schoolmaster, Franz Gruber, composed a hymn called "Song of Heaven" and sang it in church the following night. A man from a nearby town happened to hear the song, and, being impressed, memorized its words and music, which he later taught to a traveling quartet. By 1854, thirty-six years later, the piece had become so famous throughout the world that a search was undertaken for its unknown composer, and Gruber was found. The obscure and impoverished schoolmaster then learned that his song had become the most beloved church hymn of all time and that its name had been changed to "Silent Night."

Lincoln—an Athlete

Abraham Lincoln is not known today as an athlete, but in his youth he was noted as a horseman, a swimmer, a crowbar heaver, and a great jumper as well as being an expert railsplitter. He could outrun, outlift, and outwrestle any man in his county.

The Defense

Dr. Robert J. Oppenheimer, who supervised creation of the first atomic bomb, appeared before a congressional committee. They inquired of him if there was any defense against the weapon.

"Certainly," the great physicist replied.

"And that is—"

Dr. Oppenheimer looked over the hushed, expectant audience and said softly: "Peace."   —*Christian Science Monitor*

When Doctors Consult

Now when a doctor's patients are perplexed,
A consultation comes in order next—
You know what that is? In a certain place
Meet certain doctors to discuss a case
And other matters, such as weather, crops,
Potatoes, pumpkins, lager-beer, and hops.
        —*Rip Van Winkle, M.D., from Oliver Wendell Holmes*

Seven Deadly Sins

E. Stanley Jones, the famous missionary, statesman, and author-lecturer, formulated what he termed seven deadly sins: "Politics without principle; wealth without work; pleasure without conscience; knowledge without character; business without morality; science without humanity; and worship without sacrifice."

Our Most Powerful Weapon

Democracy's most powerful weapon is not a gun, tank, or bomb. It is faith—faith in brotherhood and in the dignity of men under God.   —*Harry S Truman*

What We Lose

Living in rented apartments, jamming roads and subways, punching time clocks, cramming the minds of children with technical knowledge, modern man sacrifices health of body and freedom of spirit to the scientific idol of his time. On its altar go the smell of earth, the feel of wind and weather, warmth of friendship, understanding of children, even the contemplation

of God; all these are given over to a metallic existence.
—*Charles A. Lindbergh*

Tact

Charles Schwab, former chairman of Bethlehem Steel Corporation and distinguished American industrialist, knew how to deal with men.

One day as he walked through a factory he saw three men smoking where they shouldn't have been. He did not reprimand them. He simply reached in his pocket, took out three cigars and said, "Boys, have a cigar on me, but I should appreciate it if you would not smoke it here during working hours."
—*Herbert V. Prochnow*

He Liked Himself?

The Dutch artist, Rembrandt van Rijn, painted sixty-two portraits of himself.

Disagree

Business is built by men who care enough to disagree, fight it out to the finish, get the facts. When two men always agree, one of them is unnecessary. —*William Wrigley, Jr.*

Still Around

"I'd like to be around when I'm 100 and playing in a show being staged on the moon." —*Bob Hope*

Object: Matrimony

In the middle of the last century, a prominent American newspaper carried the following classified advertisement:

"Farmer, aged 41, desires to correspond with a young woman of simple tastes. Beauty unnecessary; prettiness not desired. Object, matrimony."

A woman named Meg Charlton answered the ad, married

its author, and, as a result, eventually became first lady of the land. The advertiser was General Ulysses S. Grant, destined to be our eighteenth president.

The Facts About Government Spending

We need a campaign of education so that the public will better understand the facts of life about federal spending. We all must realize that there is no bottomless well of unlimited money in Washington. The only government money that any person can get—whether from Washington, from the city or county treasurer, or from the town selectman—must first come from the taxes he pays out of his own pocket.

—*George M. Humphrey*

No Good Loser

Nobody with gumption is what you would call a good loser. But I try to be gracious.

—*Terry Brennan, Notre Dame football coach*

His Prayer

At this moment I have in my heart a prayer. As I have assumed my heavy duties, I humbly pray to Almighty God in the words of King Solomon, "Give therefore Thy servant an understanding heart to judge Thy people that I may discern between good and bad; for who is able to judge this Thy so great a people?" I ask only to be a good and faithful servant of my Lord and my people.

—*Harry S Truman, first congressional address as president*

Our Salvation

Our salvation, and our only salvation, lies in controlling the arm of Western science by the mind of a Western philosophy guided by God's eternal truths.   —*Charles A. Lindbergh*

Self-Pity

Self-pity is our worst enemy and if we yield to it, we can never do anything wise in the world. *—Helen Keller*

A Government Bureau

One lasted thirty-six years and lost money nearly every year.
—Herbert Hoover, citing an example of "extraordinary longevity" of a government bureau.

Couldn't Deny It

When an attorney characterized Frank Lloyd Wright as America's greatest architect, Wright confessed to his wife that he could not deny it because he was under oath.

Keep It Quiet

The ancient sage who concocted the maxim "Know Thyself" might have added, "Don't Tell Anyone!" *—H. F. Henrichs*

Don't Try It

The most dangerous thing in the world is to leap a chasm in two jumps. *—David Lloyd George*

Make No Little Plans

Make no little plans; they have no magic to stir men's blood and probably themselves will not be realized. Make big plans; aim high in hope and work, remembering that a noble, logical diagram once recorded will never die, but long after we are gone will be a living thing, asserting itself with ever-growing insistency. *—Daniel Hudson Burnham, architect*

The Spirit and Mind of Man

We know that there is no true and lasting cure for world tensions in guns and bombs. We know that only the spirit and mind of man, dedicated to justice and right, can, in the long term, enable us to live in the confident tranquility that should be every man's heritage.   —*Dwight D. Eisenhower*

Difficult Secret to Keep

The most difficult secret for a man to keep is his own opinion of himself.   —*Marcel Pagnol, French playwright and author*

Sound Values

Marshall Field once indicated the follwing twelve reminders that can be helpful in obtaining a sound sense of values:

> The value of time.
> The success of perseverance.
> The pleasure of working.
> The dignity of simplicity.
> The worth of character.
> The power of kindness.
> The influence of example.
> The obligation of duty.
> The wisdom of economy.
> The virtue of patience.
> The improvement of talent.
> The joy of originating.

The Unconquerable Soul

> Out of the night that covers me,
> Black as the pit from pole to pole,
> I thank whatever gods may be
> For my unconquerable soul.

Few poems have been as widely quoted as William Ernest Henley's "Invictus." It was penned by a man who really knew physical suffering.

When only twelve years old, Henley had tuberculosis, and suffered for thirty-two years. At the age of eighteen one foot had to be amputated, in a day when painless, aseptic surgical operations were not known. A little later the doctors told the young man his other foot would have to come off.

At that time Dr. Joseph Lister was trying to convince medical men of the necessity of aseptic surgical procedure. Henley heard of the new method and went to Edinburgh to see Lister. The doctors had pronounced his case hopeless. He was practically penniless. Hopefully he appealed to the great surgeon. Lister operated and saved the foot.

Twenty months he lay on a hospital cot, racked with pain, but valiantly fighting for his life. Between the paroxysms of agony he wrote "Invictus."   —*Sunshine Magazine*

His Monument

Sir Christopher Wren, architect of St. Paul's Cathedral, London, had the following inscription in Latin carved above one of the entrances: "If you seek my monument, look around you."

Way Back in 1784

On January 16, 1784, Ben Franklin foresaw the danger of "parachute troops." He witnessed successful balloon flights over the city of Paris, and on that date he wrote to a friend in France: "It appears, as you observe, to be a discovery of great importance and what may possibly give a new turn to human affairs.... Five thousand balloons, capable of raising two men each, could not cost more than five ships of the line, and where is the prince who can afford so to cover his country with troops for its defense, as that ten thousand men descending from the clouds might not in many places do an infinite deal of mischief, before a force could be brought together to repel them?"

Common Sense

One of the grave maladies of our time is the way sophistication seems to be valued above common sense. Words cease to have the plain meaning assigned to them and become wildly elastic.

The manipulation of an idea seems to be more important than the integrity of an idea.   —*Norman Cousins*

The Guidance We Need

Belief in God and in immortality gives us the moral strength and the ethical guidance we need for virtually every action in our daily lives.   —*Wernher von Braun*

Unusual Epitaph

Thomas Jefferson composed the epitaph for his own grave. It read:

"Here was buried Thomas Jefferson, Author of the Declaration of American Independence, of the Statute of Virginia for Religious Freedom, and Father of the University of Virginia."

He neglected to mention that he was once president of the United States!

Opportunity Tried to Knock

They say opportunity knocks once, but only once. Here are a few instances when her knock was not heard.

A plumber submitted to the British War Office in 1911 a design for a tank—a then-unknown military device. Across the drawing, in red ink, was written the official comment: "This man is mad."

It is difficult to give recognition to those who loaned Robert Fulton the money for his steamboat. So fearful of ridicule were his backers that they stipulated that their names be withheld!

When George Westinghouse perfected his airbrake, in 1875, he offered it to Commodore Vanderbilt. The railroad magnate returned Westinghouse's letter, with these words across the bottom: "I have no time to waste on fools."

One day a stranger approached Mark Twain with a request for $500, for which he would sell half interest in his invention.

Twain, bit several times before, refused flatly. Out of courtesy he asked the stranger his name. "Bell," the man replied, as he turned away, "Alexander Graham Bell."

It wasn't a stranger who approached Sir Arthur Conan Doyle. A young actor playing in one of Doyle's productions suggested that he and the writer divide their incomes with one another the rest of their lives. Doyle laughed heartily. "Charlie Chaplin," he said, "if I didn't know you were joking, I'd have you fired for such audacity!"

Robert Todd Lincoln

Robert Todd Lincoln, son of President Lincoln, left Harvard law school to accept a captaincy in the Union Army. His father had invited him to attend the theater party on the eventful night when he was assassinated. Had Robert joined the party, it is likely that he would have had to sit on a stool blocking the door to the president's box, and no one could have entered.

There is something fateful about Robert Lincoln. One day he was crossing a street to tell President Garfield that he could not accept an invitation to accompany the president on a trip, when Garfield was suddenly assassinated. Again, Robert Lincoln was standing nearby when President McKinley was assassinated. Thereafter he vowed that he would never again attend a presidential function.

Dale Carnegie's Six Rules for Winning Friends

1. Be genuinely interested in other people.

2. Smile. A man without a smiling face must not open shop.

3. Remember that a man's name is to him the sweetest and most important sound in the language.

4. Be a good listener. Encourage others to talk about themselves. Many persons call a doctor when all they want is an audience.

5. Talk in terms of the other man's interest.

6. Make the other person feel important—and do it with sincerity.

Herbert Hoover's Bill of Rights for Boys

1. Like everybody else, a boy has a right to the pursuit of happiness.

2. He has a right to play so that he may stretch his imagination and prove his prowess and skill.

3. He has a right to the constructive joys of adventure and the thrills that are a part of an open life.

4. He has a right to affection and friendship.

5. He has a right to the sense of security in belonging to some group.

6. He has a right to health protections that will make him an inch taller than his dad.

7. He has a right to the education and training that will amplify his own natural bents, and fit him into a job.

8. And I would add another right—the right to accept the obligations of citizenship in a democracy—perhaps the greatest right a boy, or anyone else, can have.

Warnings

Some 2,000 years ago, Plutarch warned: "The real destroyer of the liberties of people is he who spreads among them bounties, donations, and benefits."

An old French peasant made this sad observation after the collapse of France in World War II (France was burdened with social subsidies): "My country fell because we had come to consider France a cow to be milked—not a watchdog to feed."

Coolidge Saved Time

When Calvin Coolidge was president, he saw dozens of people each day. Most had complaints of one kind or another. A visiting governor once told the president that he did not understand how he could see so many people in the space of a few hours. "Why, you are finished with them by dinner time," the governor remarked, "while I'm often at my desk until midnight."

"Yes," said Coolidge, "but you talk back."

War

I confess without shame that I am tired and sick of the war. Its glory is all moonshine. Even victory the most brilliant is over dead and mangled bodies, the anguish and lamentation of distant families crying to me for missing sons, husbands, and fathers. It is only those who have not heard the shrieks and groans of the wounded and lacerated, that clamor for more blood, more vengance, more desolation.

—*William Tecumseh Sherman, American general*

No Little Thing

Mark Twain told of the time his little girl broke her doll, and he attempted to quiet her sobbing by making light of the incident. "You shouldn't cry over a little thing like that." But she, looking up through her tears, asked: "Daddy, what is a little thing?" and he was unable to answer, for her broken doll was as important to her as a kingdom to a monarch.

The Piano Said "Do"

Alexander Bell was experimenting with his new invention, the telephone. The research required money, and he had none. His invention sounded so impossible. nobody was willing to back it.

Bell went to see a man by the name of Hubbard, in Cambridge. Hubbard was rich and Bell hoped to interest him in his invention. But Bell knew it would be unwise to attempt to sell him on the "impossible" idea of making a voice go over a wire.

Bell was as good a salesman as he was inventor. He sat down and played Hubbard's piano for a while. Then he looked at Hubbard and said, "Do you know that I can make this piano sing?"

Hubbard was interested, but skeptical. Bell depressed the pedal, sang "do," and the piano wires vibrated back, "do." Then, as he explained how he had done it, he described his own discovery, the harmonic principle of voice transmission.

Hubbard backed his project.   —*Sunshine Magazine*

More to Life

There is more to life than increasing its speed.
                                               —*Mahatma Gandhi*

Admiral Hyman G. Rickover on Life

If I had to choose between being forthright and candid and intellectually honest or keeping this job, I would select the former.

Changes are not accomplished without resistance or completed without reaction.

Happiness comes from the full use of one's power to achieve excellence. Life is potentially an empty hole, and there are few more satisfying ways of fulfilling it than by achieving and exercising excellence.

Creativity is a basic principle of existence which helps to give purpose in life. The deepest joy in life is to be creative. To find an undeveloped situation, to see the possibilities, to decide upon a course of action, and then devote the whole of one's resources to carry it out, even if it means battling against the stream of contemporary opinion, is a satisfaction in comparison with which superficial pleasures are trivial.

Trying to make things work in government is sometimes like trying to sew buttons on a custard pie.

No one can be forced to render an account for doing nothing.

To have courage means to pursue your goals, or to satisfy your responsibilities, even though others stand in the way and success seems like a dream. It takes courage to stand and fight for what you believe is right. And the fight never ends. You have to start it over again each morning as the sun rises.

Laughter

Laughter is the shortest distance between two people.
—Victor Borge

Always in Search

The Good Shepherd is always in search of the lost sheep.
—Bishop Fulton J. Sheen

Heredity

Heredity is an omnibus in which all our ancestors ride, and every now and then one of them puts his head out and embarrasses us. *—Oliver Wendell Holmes*

His Philosophy of Life

The best thing to give to your enemy is forgiveness; to an opponent, tolerance; to a friend, your heart; to your child, a good example; to a father, deference; to your mother, conduct that will make her proud of you; to yourself, respect; to all men, charity. *—Arthur James Balfour*

The Reward

No person was ever honored for what he received. Honor has been the reward for what he gave. *—Calvin Coolidge*

The Human Race

Such is the human race. Often it does seem such a pity that Noah ... didn't miss the boat. *—Mark Twain*

October

October is the month for painted leaves.... As fruits and leaves and the day itself acquire a bright tint just before they fall, so the year near its setting. October is its sunset sky; November the later twilight.   *—Henry David Thoreau*

Vice or Virtue

Extremism in the defense of liberty is no vice.... Moderation in the pursuit of justice is no virtue.   *—Barry Goldwater*

A Short Memory

Nothing is so admirable in politics as a short memory.
—John Kenneth Galbraith

The Same All Over

Politicians are the same all over. They promise to build a bridge even where there is no river.   *—Nikita Khrushchev*

Innocent Employment

There are few ways in which a man can be more innocently employed than in getting money.   *—Dr. Samuel Johnson*

Irish: Eloquent

My one claim to originality among Irishmen is that I have never made a speech.   *—George Moore*

Ignorant Enough

Joe ... was ignorant enough to feel superior to everything.
—John Ciardi

It's Difficult

The hardest job kids face today is learning good manners without seeing any.   —*Fred Astaire*

His Concern

I don't know who my grandfather was; I am much more concerned to know what his grandson will be.   —*Abraham Lincoln*

Napoleon's Philosophy

The word impossible is not in my dictionary.
—*Napoleon Bonaparte*

Conceited

He is a self-made man and worships his creator.
—*John Bright, referring to Disraeli*

Whose Fault

Now when I bore people at a party they think it's their fault.
—*Henry Kissinger*

Humor

Humor makes the educated mind a safer mind.

Chapter 6

THOUGHTFUL COMMENTS ON IMPORTANT SUBJECTS

Crowds Never

Individuals are occasionally guided by reason, crowds never.   *—Dean W. R. Inge*

A Good Rule

When in doubt, tell the truth.   *—Mark Twain*

No Successful Liar

No man has a memory long enough to be a successful liar.   *—Abraham Lincoln*

When Truth Is Violated

Truth is not only violated by falsehood; it may be equally outraged by silence.

—Henry Frederic Amiel

The Strongest Argument

The truth is always the strongest argument.   —*Sophocles*

Building a Nation

We cannot bring prosperity by discouraging thrift. We cannot strengthen the weak by weakening the strong. We cannot help small men by tearing down big men. We cannot help the poor by ignoring the rich. We cannot lift the wage earner by pulling down the wage payer. We cannot keep out of trouble by spending more than our income.   —*The Better Way*

The Measure of a Person

The measure of a person is not the number of people who serve him, but the number of the people he serves.

Take Time to Decide

Set aside a little time once a year, at least, to decide where you are going, what are your priorities, ambitions, aspirations. Not just in your business alone, but also in the personal things—your own free evenings, your own feelings of status and worthwhileness in life, and your own dignity, your own integrity, your family.   —*William C. Menninger*

An Open Heart

There is dew in one flower and not in another, because one opens its cup and takes it in, while the other closes itself, and the dewdrops run off. God rains his goodness and mercy as widespread as the dew, and if we lack them, it is because we will not open our hearts to receive them.

—*Henry Ward Beecher*

Democracy

Democracy means not "I am as good as you are," but "You are as good as I am."   —*Theodore Parker*

How to Live

But when thou makest a feast, call the poor, the maimed, the lame, the blind: and thou shalt be blessed.   —*Luke 14:13*

Father to Son

Advice from a father to his son: "My boy, treat everybody with politeness, even those who are rude to you. For remember that you show courtesy to others not because they are gentlemen, but because you are one."

Success

Hard work means nothing to a hen. She just keeps on digging worms and laying eggs, regardless of what the business prognosticators say about the outlook for the year. If the ground is hard, she scratches harder. If it's dry, she digs deeper. If it's wet, she digs where it's dry. If she strikes a rock, she digs around it. If she gets a few more hours of daylight, she gives a few more eggs and digs a few hours longer. Did you ever see a pessimistic hen? Did you ever hear one cackle because work was hard? Not on your life! They save their breath for digging and the cackles come for eggs. Success means digging!

—*Good Reading*

What Everyone Likes to Be Told

Never be sparing with words of appreciation, especially when they are deserved by those around us. Everyone likes to be told that they are admired, respected, appreciated, and even liked.

The First Duty

The first duty toward children is to make them happy. If you have not made them happy, you have wronged them; no other good they may get can make up for that.   —*Charles Buxton*

Greatness

The great man is to be the servant of mankind, not they of him. —*Theodore Parker*

Character

A man's character is the reality of himself. His reputation is the opinion others have formed of him. Character is in him; reputation is from other people—that is the substance, this is the shadow. —*Henry Ward Beecher*

He Likes Autumn

I like spring, but it is too young. I like summer, but it is too proud. So I like best of all autumn, because its leaves are a little yellow, its tone mellower, its colors richer, and it is tinged a little with sorrow.... Its golden richness speaks not of the innocence of spring, nor of the power of summer, but of the mellowness and kindly wisdom of approaching age. It knows the limitations of life and is content. —*Lin Yutang*

Few Have Imagination

The opportunities of man are limited by only his imagination. But so few have imagination that there are ten thousand fiddlers to one composer. —*Charles F. Kettering*

Originality

Originality, I fear, is too often only undetected and frequently unconscious plagiarism. —*William Inge*

What a Father Can Do

The most important thing a father can do for his children is to demonstrate his love and admiration for their mother.

The Purpose of Education

The purpose of education is to transmit the culture of a society to its young. In accomplishing this, it is hoped that the individual will be armed with knowledge, strength of judgement and moral virtues, as well as the ability to make a living, and in the process, preserve the heritage of the nation and the achievements of previous generations.   —*George S. Benson*

Love of Country

I think we do need to go back to patriotism and love of country instead of trying to tear it down.   —*James H. Howard,*
World War II ace and
Medal of Honor winner

Reputation and Character

A person's reputation is precious, but a person's character is priceless.

Lincoln's Conviction

I can see how it might be possible for a man to look down upon the earth and be an atheist, but I cannot conceive how he could look up into the heavens and say there is no God.
—*Abraham Lincoln*

What He Believed

I believe in the sacredness of a promise, that a man's word should be as good as his bond; that character—not wealth or power or position—is of supreme worth.
—*John D. Rockefeller, Jr.*

Our Homes

Centuries before there was a state, or a school, or a church, homes were instituted as places where men and women should live together in love and happiness; where children should be reared into worthy lives. But many enemies threaten the home today—disrespect, disloyalty, lack of Christian atmosphere, little religious training, little or no Christian literature. Many parents have become lax in their discipline; in their fear of being old-fashioned, they are permitting their children to do things that are not only questionable, but often demoralizing and dangerous.

Our homes need to get back to God's standard. We need to exalt the sacredness of the marriage tie; we need to make our homes a place of sobriety, and uprightness, and unfailing love. This sacred institution should be filled with honor and righteousness, that no stranger need ask, "Does God live here?"

—Sunshine Magazine

Man Will Prevail

I believe that man will not merely endure, he will prevail ... because he has a soul, a spirit capable of compassion and sacrifice and endurance.   *—William Faulkner*

Not Easy

A child should always say what's true
And speak when he is spoken to,
And behave mannerly at table;
At least as far as he is able.   *—Robert Louis Stevenson*

Constant Trials

We are always in the forge, or on the anvil; by trials God is shaping us for higher things.   *—Henry Ward Beecher*

Circumstances

Man is not the creature of circumstances; circumstances are the creatures of man.   *—Benjamin Disraeli*

Most Valuable

The most valuable thing I have learned from life is to regret nothing. —*Somerset Maugham*

Concentrate

Do what you love. Know your own bone; gnaw at it, bury it, unearth it and gnaw it still. —*Henry David Thoreau*

New Ideas

If you want to succeed you should strike out on new paths rather than travel the worn paths of accepted success.
—*John D. Rockefeller*

The Years Teach One

The years teach much which the days never know.
—*Ralph Waldo Emerson*

Modesty in Everyone

In his private heart no man much respects himself.
—*Mark Twain*

God

We have been the recipients of the choicest bounties of Heaven; we have grown in numbers, wealth and power as no other nation has ever grown. But we have forgotten God. We have forgotten the gracious hand which preserved us in peace and multiplied and enriched and strengthened us;' and we have vainly imagined, in the deceitfulness of our hearts, that all these blessings were produced by some superior wisdom and virtue of our own. Intoxicated with unbroken success, we have become too self-sufficient to feel that necessity of redeeming and preserving grace, too proud to pray to the God that made us. —*Abraham Lincoln*

Dreams

We grow by dreams. All big men are dreamers. They see things in the soft haze of a spring day, or in the red fire of a long winter's evening. Some of us let these great dreams die, but others nourish and protect them, nurse them through bad days till they bring them to the light which comes always to those who sincerely hope that their dreams will come true.

—Woodrow Wilson

His View of Life

The longer I live, the more beautiful life becomes.

—Frank Lloyd Wright

The Greatest Victory

Self-conquest is the greatest of all victories.   *—Plato*

Mother

A man takes counsel with his wife; he obeys his mother.

—Aimi Martin

Let France have good mothers and she will have good sons.

—Napoleon Bonaparte

A mother is not to lean on but to make leaning unnecessary.

—Dorothy Fisher

All that I am or hope to be I owe to my angel mother.

—Abraham Lincoln

What the Cynic Sees

The cynic is one who never sees a good quality in a man, and never fails to see a bad one. He is the human owl, vigilant in darkness and blind to light, mousing for vermin, and never seeing noble game. The cynic puts all human actions into two classes—openly bad and secretly bad.   *—Henry Ward Beecher*

Ideas

The man with a new idea is a crack until the idea succeeds.

—Mark Twain

True Greatness

Men and women of rich attainments and ability are usually modest and unassuming, while the empty-headed people all too often feverishly lift themselves above the crowd as if afraid they may not receive the attention they think they deserve. One of the surest evidences of true greatness is a humble spirit.

—The Uplift

Fate of the World

Upon our children—how they are taught—rests the fate or fortune of tomorrow's world.   *—B. C. Forbes*

A Big Difference

We're told you'll never find the line "Money is the root of all evil" in the Bible. But you will find that it states, "Love of money is the root of all evil." There's a big difference.

Using Circumstances

The ideal man bears the accidents of life with dignity and grace, making the best of circumstances.   *—Aristotle*

Determination

A determined soul will do more with a rusty monkey wrench than a loafer will accomplish with all the tools in a machine shop.   *—Rupert Hughes*

What Would You Have If You Reached Your Goal?

In a little country community a farmer had a dog who spent

part of his time sitting by the side of a main-traveled highway waiting for big trucks. When the dog saw a large truck come around the corner, he would get ready, and as the truck passed him he would take out after it down the road, barking and doing his best to overtake it.

One day the farmer's neighbor said, "Sam, do you think that hound of yours is ever going to catch a truck?"

"Well, Bill," Sam replied, "that isn't what worries me. What worries me is what he would do if he caught one!"

Many of us in life are like that hound. We give our lives pursuing goals that have little value even if we reach them. Sometimes it pays to stop and ask whether we have objectives worth pursuing.   —*Herbert V. Prochnow*

Making the Best of It

There are no circumstances, however unfortunate, that clever people do not extract some advantage from.
                                    —*François La Rochefoucauld*

The Oyster

Men of mettle turn disappointments into helps, as the oyster turns into pearls the sand which annoys it.
                                    —*Orison Swett Marden*

Learning from Failure

Failure is instructive. The person who really thinks learns quite as much from his failures as from his successes.
                                    —*John Dewey*

Problems

Problems are opportunities and there are a lot of them around.
                                    —*Arnold Glasow*

Trouble

Opportunity wears many disguises, including trouble.

—*Frank Tyger*

Plausible and Wrong

There is always an easy solution to every human problem—neat, plausible, and wrong. —*H. L. Mencken*

The Present Hour

One of the illusions of life is that the present hour is not the critical, decisive hour. Write it on your heart that every day is the best day of the year. He only is rich who owns the day, and no one owns the day who allows it to be invaded with worry, fret and anxiety. Finish every day, and be done with it. You have done what you could. —*Ralph Waldo Emerson*

Writing Is Easy

Writing is easy. All you do is stare at a blank sheet of paper until drops of blood form on your forehead. —*Gene Fowler*

Three Things Necessary

Three things are necessary for the salvation of man: to know what he ought to believe, to know what he ought to desire, and to know what he ought to do. —*St. Thomas Aquinas*

Freedom

According to a story told of Karl Marx's widow, she used to say to him: "Dear, I wish you spent less time writing about capital and a little more time making it." Well, of course if he had done that, the world would have been saved a great deal of trouble. But he was fortunate. He lived in Britain, where the freedom that is the breath of life to us enabled him to write the kind of things he would never have been able to write under the system he espoused.

Serving Others

I don't know what your destiny will be, but one thing I know;
the only ones among you who will be really happy are those
who have sought and found how to serve.   —*Albert Schweitzer*

Your Viewpoint

We think too small. Like the frog at the bottom of the well.
He thinks the sky is only as big as the top of the well. If he
surfaced, he would have an entirely different view.

—*Mao Tse-Tung*

The Eternal Rules

There is no truth more thoroughly established than that there
exists in the economy and course of nature an indissoluble union
between virtue and happiness, between duty and advantage. The
propitious smiles of Heaven can never be expected on a nation
that disregards the eternal rules of order and right, which Heaven
itself has ordained.   —*George Washington*

The Best Foreign Policy

Honesty is also the best foreign policy.   —*Herbert V. Prochnow*

The Shortcomings of Others

Too many of us become enraged because we have to bear the
shortcomings of others. We should remember that not one of
us is perfect, and that others see our defects as obviously as
we see theirs. We forget too often to look at ourselves through
the eyes of our friends. Let us, therefore, bear the shortcomings
of each other for the ultimate benefit of everyone.

—*Abraham Lincoln*

Thinking

Few people think more than two or three times a year. I have made an international reputation for myself by thinking once or twice a week. —*George Bernard Shaw*

The Misfortune

No one is exempt from talking nonsense, the misfortune is to do it solemnly. —*Michel de Montaigne*

Giving

We should give as we would receive, cheerfully, quickly and without hesitation, for there is no grace in a benefit that sticks to the fingers. —*Seneca*

You Gain

What is done for another is done for oneself. —*Paulus*

Still Learning

I am still learning. —*Michelangelo*

Reality

One of the criteria of emotional maturity is having the ability to deal constructively with reality. —*William C. Menninger*

Not So Great

Once infatuated with our unprecedented achievements, men are now appalled by the realization history is big enough to swallow them up too. —*Hermann Joseph Muller*

When We Are Wrong

A man should never be ashamed to own he has been in the wrong, which is but saying in other words, that he is wiser today than he was yesterday. —*Alexander Pope*

For Others

Everyone has a code of ethics for everyone.   —*Robert Half*

Just Forget

Be a good forgetter. Forget the things that are behind; forget injuries, slights, unkind words; be too big to be hurt; be too great to be unkind; be too busy to quarrel; too wise to engage in unseemly gossip; too strong to permit little annoyances to turn you from life's big road; too clean to stain your character with any kind of muckraking.   —*Good Reading*

Moments of Prayer

Certain thoughts are prayers. There are moments when, whatever be the attitude of the body, the soul is on its knees.

—*Victor Hugo*

Only Once

I expect to pass through this world but once. Any good, therefore, that I can do, or any kindness that I can show to any fellow creature, let me do it now. Let me not defer or neglect it, for I shall not pass this way again.   —*Stephen Grellet*

Great Men

That nation has not lived in vain which has given the world Washington and Lincoln, the best great men and the greatest good men whom history can show.   —*Henry Cabot Lodge*

Free to Argue

It is not necessary to understand things in order to argue about them.   —*Pierre Augustin de Beaumarchais*

What Adversity Does

Adversity reminds men of religion.   —*Livy*

Most of Us

The mass of men lead lives of quiet desperation.
                                    —*Henry David Thoreau*

Concise View

The business of America is business.   —*Calvin Coolidge*

From the Heart

In friendship we find nothing false or insincere; everything is straightforward and springs from the heart.   —*Cicero*

Your Character

A man never discloses his own character so clearly as when he describes another's.   —*Jean Paul Richter*

A Nuisance

It is a nuisance that knowledge can only be acquired by hard work.   —*Somerset Maugham*

Webster's View

If we abide by the principles taught in the Bible, our country will go on prospering.   —*Daniel Webster*

Life

To lengthen thy life, lessen thy meals.   —*Benjamin Franklin*

Ideas

For an idea that does not at first seem insane, there is no hope. —*Albert Einstein*

A Good Reputation

The way to gain a good reputation is to endeavor to be what you desire to appear. —*Socrates*

Atomic Age

The Atomic Age is here to stay—but are we? —*Bennett Cerf*

The Greatest Medicine

Me retire? I'd die before I'd give up hearing an audience laugh. It's the greatest tonic, the greatest medicine, in the world.
—*Bob Hope*

The Reason

Few men are lacking in capacity, but they fail because they are lacking in application. —*Calvin Coolidge*

A Great Legacy

Books are the legacies that a great genius leaves to mankind, which are delivered down from generation to generation, as presents to the posterity of those who are yet unborn.
—*Joseph Addison*

Patriotism and the Size of the Flag

The size of the flag we wave is not a true measure of our patriotism.

The Meaning of Democracy

Democracy substitutes election by the incompetent many for appointment by the corrupt few. —*George Bernard Shaw*

Old Age

The harvest of old age is the memory and rich store of blessings laid up in earlier life. —*Cicero*

Beauty

When the candles are out all women are fair. —*Plutarch*

Having a Home

My parents spent a lot of time with us and made us feel loved. The feeling of having a home base was strong.
—*Walter Payton, Chicago Bears football player*

With the Years

Nobody ever outgrows Scripture; the book widens and deepens with our years. —*Charles Haddon Spurgeon*

An Essential Condition

In business, the earning of profit is something more than an incident of success. It is an essential condition of success. It is an essential condition of success because the continued absence of profit itself spells failure. —*Justice Louis D. Brandeis*

The Caliber of a Person

The caliber of a person is to be found in the ability to meet disappointment and be enriched rather than embittered by it.

Management

Management by objectives works if you know the objectives. Ninety percent of the time you don't.   —*Peter Drucker*

What the Bible Teaches

The Scriptures teach us the best way of living, the noblest way of suffering, and the most comfortable way of dying.
—*John Flavel*

The Way to a Man's Heart

The royal road to a man's heart is to talk to him about the things he treasures most.   —*Dale Carnegie*

The Real Test

Profitability is the sovereign criterion of the enterprise.
—*Peter Drucker*

Naturally

It is one of the most beautiful compensations of life that no man can sincerely try to help another without helping himself.
—*William Shakespeare*

The Same Problems

Human nature will not change. In any future great national trial, compared with the men of this, we shall have as weak and as strong, as silly and as wise, as bad and as good.
—*Abraham Lincoln*

Delay

The greatest remedy for anger is delay.   —*Seneca*

Where God Is Found

God is found in two places; one of his dwellings is Heaven, and the other is in a meek and thankful heart.

Friendship

You can buy real friendship with friendship, but never with dollars.

Money

Light purse, heavy heart.   *—Benjamin Franklin*

What Art Does

Without art, the crudeness of reality would make the world unbearable.   *—George Bernard Shaw*

God's Revelation

The Bible is God's revelation to man, his guide, his light.
—Alfred Armand Montapert

How Short Life Is

When thou art above measure angry, bethink thee how momentary is man's life.   *—Marcus Aurelius*

Time Is Flying

> Gather ye rose-buds while ye may,
> Old Time is still a-flying:
> And this same flower that smiles today,
> Tomorrow will be dying.   *—Robert Herrick*

Ability

Natural ability without education has more often raised a man to glory and virtue than education without natural ability.

—Cicero

Loving One's Neighbor

It is easier to love humanity as a whole than to love one's neighbor.
—Eric Hoffer

When We Believe

We are inclined to believe those we do not know, because they have never deceived us.   *—Samuel Johnson*

Progress

To be conscious that you are ignorant is a great step toward knowledge.

Everything But

Money can buy you everything but happiness and pay your fare to every place but heaven.

A Hard Teacher

Experience is a hard teacher because she gives the test first, the lesson afterward.

The Real Test

There is no better test for a man's ultimate integrity than his behavior when he is wrong.

Why Is It?

Why is it in a civilized nation that happiness and intelligence are so seldom found together?   *—Herbert V. Prochnow*

Head Table!

Here is where speakers take their seat, pleased to be looked at, too scared to eat. —*Richard Armour*

Greatest Joy

An old Chinese philosopher was asked what was the greatest joy he had found in life. "A child," he said, "going down the road singing after asking me the way."

—*Bulletin,* Mansfield, Ohio

It Isn't Easy

To be poor without being resentful is difficult; to be rich without being arrogant is even harder.

What We Need to Learn

In modern times, man has learned how to split the atom and build planes that conquer space and distance and bring people the world over within hours and minutes of each other; yet man has not been able to find a formula that enables men of different races, cultures, personalities, and religions to live together amicably.

Ominous Sounds

In world affairs, nothing sounds so ominous as the rumbling of empty stomachs.

Silence May Be Wisdom

Silence at the proper season is wisdom, and better than any speech. —*Plutarch*

What We Value

What men value in this world is not rights but privileges.

—*H. L. Mencken*

Discipline

Who is tampering with the soul of America? There is rot and there is blight and there is cutting and filling to be done if we, as the leaders of free men, are to survive the hammer blows which quite plainly are in store for us all.

We have reached the point where we should examine the debilitating philosophy of permissiveness. Let this not be confused with the philosophy of liberty. The school system that permits our children to develop a quarter of their natural talents is not a champion of our liberties. The playwright who would degrade us, the author who would profit from pandering to the worst that is in us, are no friends of ours.

It is time we hit the sawdust trail. It is time we revived the idea that there is such a thing as sin—just plain old willful sin. It is time we brought self-discipline back into style in America.
—*Jenkin Lloyd Jones, editor,* Tribune *(Tulsa, Oklahoma)*

Youth in Old Age

Old age is not a disease. Because a person is old, he is not inadequate. There is youth in old age, and beauty too, if we only have the eyes to see.

The Difference?

If a man sits all day on the bank of a lake with a pole in his hand, people respect him for being a "patient fisherman." If he sits on his porch thinking things over, he is referred to as "that lazy old fellow down the street."

Civilization

Civlization is a stream with banks. The stream is sometimes filled with blood from people killing, stealing, shouting and doing things historians usually record, while on the banks, unnoticed, people build homes, make love, raise children, sing songs, write poetry and even whittle statues. The story of civilization is the story of what happened on the banks. Historians are pessimists because they ignore the banks for the river.

—Will and Ariel Durant

Your Life

Every life is a work of art, shaped by the person who lives it.

Letters Without Learning

It is possible for a student to win twelve letters at a university without his learning how to write one.

—Robert Maynard Hutchins

Same Value

The conservative who resists change is as valuable as the radical who proposes it. *—Will and Ariel Durant*

Greatness

It takes a great man to make a good listener.

—Sir Arthur Helps

Rights and Obligations

With every civil right there has to be a corresponding civil obligation. *—Edison Haines*

Our Age

Perfection of means and confusion of ends seem to characterize our age. *—Albert Einstein*

The Pledge of Allegiance

The Pledge of Allegiance to the flag was adopted by Congress in the summer of 1892. The pledge is:

I pledge allegiance to the Flag of the United States of America and to the Republic for which it stands, one nation under God, indivisible, with Liberty and Justice for All.

The words "Under God" were approved by Congress in 1954. When President Eisenhower signed the act, adding the recognition of God, he said, "In this way we are reaffirming the transcendence of religious faith in America's heritage and future; in this way we shall constantly strengthen those spiritual weapons which forever will be our country's most powerful resource in peace and war."

Prayer and Life

They who pray as they ought, will endeavor to live as they pray.

Costs Too Much

That laughter costs too much that is purchased by the sacrifice of decency.

Our Heritage

The practical thing we can do, if we really want to make the world over again, is to try out the word "old" for a while. There are some "old" things that made this country.

There is the "old" virtue of religious faith. There are the "old" virtues of complete integrity, loyalty, and truthfulness.

There is the "old" virtue of incorruptible service and honor in public office.

There are the "old" virtues of economy in government, of self-reliance, thrift, and individual liberty.

There are the "old" virtues of patriotism, real love of country, and willingness to sacrifice for it.

These "old" ideas are very inexpensive. They even would help win hot and cold wars. Some of these "old" things are slipping badly in American life. And if they slip too far, the lights will go out of America, even if we win the hot and cold wars. Think about it. —*Herbert Hoover*

Many of Us Do

Don't make the mistake of letting yesterday use up too much of today.

No Less Important

The prayers a person lives on his feet are no less important than those he says on his knees.

An Important Voice

What a father says to his children is not heard by the world, but it will be heard by posterity.

The Power of Example

There is a transcendent power in example. We reform others unconsciously, when we walk uprightly.

The Importance of the Family

No nation can be destroyed while it possesses a good home life.

Famous Inscriptions

Over one of the doors of the Milan cathedral is sculptured a cross beneath which are the words: "All that troubles is but for a moment." Under the great central entrance in the main aisle is the inscription: "That only is important which is eternal."

Easier

It's not easy to run a home. It's easier to go down to the filling station, sit on a bench, and run the country.

Keeps Coming Back

Kindness is a hard thing to give away. It keeps coming back to the giver.

How to Forget Troubles

A good way to forget your troubles is to help others out of theirs.

Conceit

Conceit is a closer companion of ignorance than of learning.

Talent and Character

Talent is built in solitude; character in the stream of the world.
                                                                    —*Goethe*

The Ultimate Purpose

The ultimate purpose of man is not merely to fly from Chicago to London in seven hours—eating a ten-course dinner en route. The great goal of free men is not simply to create a sleek and self-satisfied culture of comfort, leisure, and fun.... The final measure of greatness is whether you and I have increased the freedom of man, enhanced his dignity, and brought him nearer to the nobility of the divine image in which he was created.
                                                    —*Herbert V. Prochnow*

Deceptive Security

Both fear and self-satisfaction lock men's minds against fresh ideas. For, however false, in acceptance of the status quo there is seeming comfort and deceptive security. But the mere defense of a fixed position is negative and static. One cannot glide into the future without leaving the comfortable cliches and familiar axioms of the past.   —*Philip Will, Jr., architect*

Character and Reputation

Character is like a tree and reputation like its shadow. The shadow is what we think of it; the tree is the real thing.

—Abraham Lincoln

Fair Play and Self-Restraint

The ideas of fair play and self-restraint are essentially religious. They help keep dog-eat-dog practices in check and enable the business system to operate without strict governmental control; self-restraint rather than legal restraint is the rule. The typical emphasis on individual responsibility is another example of a basically religious idea which permeates American life, including business life. *—James C. Worthy*

The Beacon Light

Our Republic serves as the beacon light of hope throughout the world, and it does so because, uniquely among the systems of government that have been devised, it maximizes human freedom. *—John E. Swearingen*

The Value of Work

I cannot imagine life without work. It needn't be a professional career or a factory job. Staying home and raising a family can be hard work, too. This mad scramble for leisure time says something about our values. Somewhere along the line, work has picked up a bad name. I'd like to see it gain the respectability and prestige it once enjoyed. It's what made this country great.

—Ann Landers, newspaper columnist

Today

Today is your day and mine, the only day we have, the day in which we play our part. What our part may signify in the great whole, we may not understand; but we are here to play it, and now is our time. *—David Starr Jordan*

Salvation

Longfellow could take a sheet of paper, write a poem on it and make it worth sixty thousand dollars. That is talent. Rockefeller could sign a piece of paper and make it worth millions. That is capital. A mechanic can take material worth $5 and make it into an article worth $50. That is skill. A merchant can buy an article for eighty cents, put it on his counter and sell it for a dollar. That is business.

God can take a worthless, sinful life, wash it, cleanse it, put his Holy Spirit within it and make it a blessing to all humanity. That is salvation. —*Author unknown*

Only One Message

In a world in which we are overwhelmed with a blizzard of messages, we can easily lose sight of which messages are really important. But, realistically there is only one message that can never be ignored. It is the message of God, the one message which gives meaning to all others. Read the Bible and encourage others to do so. It's got a message for each of us.

—*William M. Ellinghaus, president,*
American Telephone &
Telegraph

The Problem

Most of God's troubles with laborers in his vineyard can be traced to absenteeism. —*The Protestant Voice*

Government

An empty stomach is not a good political adviser.

—*Albert Einstein*

Aims

The great thing in this world is not so much where we are, but in what direction we are going. —*Oliver Wendell Holmes*

Democracy

Democracy is based on the conviction that there are extraordinary possibilities in ordinary people.   —*Harry Emerson Fosdick*

Livelihood

He that hath a trade, hath an estate. He that hath a calling, hath an office of profit and honor.   —*Benjamin Franklin*

True Wisdom

The wise know too well their own weakness to assume infallibility; and he who knows most, knows how little he knows.
—*Thomas Jefferson*

Goals

To be what we are and to become what we are capable of becoming, is the only end of life.   —*Robert Louis Stevenson*

Habit

Habit is a cable; we weave a thread of it each day, and at last we cannot break it.   —*Horace Mann*

What Difficulties Do

If there were no difficulties, there would be no triumphs.

Never Lost

No opportunity is ever lost; someone else picks up those you miss.

Hope

There has always been a sunrise after a sunset.

Expect Changes in Your Friends

The only man who behaved sensibly was my tailor; he took my measure anew every time he saw me, whilst all the rest went on with their old measurements and expected them to fit me.   —*George Bernard Shaw*

To Be Contented

It is right to be contented with what we have, never with what we are.   —*Sir James Mackintosh*

Selfishness

Selfishness is the great unknown sin. No selfish person ever thought himself selfish.   —*Southern Churchman*

Three Steps Hard to Climb

The first step is to think kindly of one's neighbor. The second is to speak kindly of him. The third is to act kindly toward him. The reason the steps are hard to climb is that we are too busily engaged in thinking well of ourselves, speaking well of ourselves, and acting in a manner that we think will do ourselves the most good.

The Duty of Every Citizen

I believe it to be the duty of every citizen to do all within his power to improve the conditions under which men work and live. I believe that that man renders the greatest social service who so co-operates in the organization of industry as to afford the largest number of men the greatest opportunity for self-development, and the enjoyment by every man of those benefits which his own work adds to the wealth of civilization.

—*John D. Rockefeller, Jr.*

A Prayer

Lord, make me an instrument of Thy Peace. Where there is hatred, let me sow love, where there is injury, pardon; whence there is doubt, faith; where there is despair, hope; where there is darkness, light; and where there is sickness, joy. O Divine Master, grant that I may not so much seek to be consoled as to console; to be understood as to understand; to be loved as to love; for it is in giving that we receive; it is in pardoning that we are pardoned; and it is in dying that we are born to eternal life.   —*St. Francis of Assisi*

Common Weakness

Man's most pitiful weakness is his desire to get something for nothing.   —*Friendly Cheer*

Luxury Loving

Man is a luxury-loving animal. His greatest exertions are made in pursuit not of necessities but of superfluities.   —*Eric Hoffer*

Wanting to Win

Winning isn't everything—but wanting to win is.
—*Vince Lombardi*

Either Way

The one function that TV news performs very well is that when there is no news we give it to you with the same emphasis as if there were news.   —*David Brinkley*

The Difference

An optimist sees an opportunity in every calamity; a pessimist sees a calamity in every opportunity.   —*Winston Churchill*

Experience

Experience is not what happens to a man. It is what a man does with what happens to him.   —*Aldous Huxley*

What He Believes

For my part I believe in the forgiveness of sin and the redemption of ignorance.   —*Adlai Stevenson*

The Biggest Mistake

The biggest mistake is the fear that you will make one.

It's Disguised

Only a comparative few recognize opportunity because it is disguised as hard work.

Our Task

Our task now is not to fix the blame for the past, but to fix the course for the future.   —*John F. Kennedy*

Why Nations Decline and Fall

Edward Gibbon, in 1788, set forth in his famous book *Decline and Fall of the Roman Empire* five basic reasons why that great civilization withered and died.

1. The undermining of the dignity and sanctity of the home, which is the basis for human society.

2. Higher and higher taxes: the spending of public money for free bread and circuses for the populace.

3. The mad craze for pleasure, with sports and plays becoming more exciting, more brutal, and more immoral.

4. The building of great armaments when the real enemy was within—decay of individual responsibility.

5. The decay of religion, whose leaders lost touch with life and their power to guide.

The Right Way to Live

Constantly speak the truth, boldly rebuke vice, and patiently suffer for the truth's sake. —*The Book of Common Prayer*

The Long Road of History

The long road of history is lined with the ruins of nations which bought the souls of their peoples with the lure of a granted security, and then led them to ruin by that mirage. Security that is real and enduring is attained only by peoples who will accept their responsibility as duties to themselves and their fellows, and ask only that the State guard the avenues of freedom and keep them open. —*Dr. Russell J. Clinchy*

A Good Life

Do not worry. Eat three square meals a day, say your prayers, be courteous to your creditors, keep your digestion good, steer clear of biliousness, exercise, go slow, and go easy. Maybe there are other things that your special case requires to make you happy, but, my friend, these I reckon will give you a good life.

—*Abraham Lincoln*

The Rewards of Maturity

The belief that youth is the happiest time of life is founded on a fallacy. The happiest person is the person who thinks the most interesting thoughts.... As we advance in years we really grow happier, if we live intelligently.... To say that youth is happier than maturity is like saying that the view from the bottom of the tower is better than the view from the top. As we ascend, the range of our view widens immensely; the horizon is pushed farther away. Finally as we reach the summit it is as if we had the world at our feet. —*William Lyon Phelps*

Reading Enriches

It is not true that we have only one life to live; if we can read, we can live as many more lives and as many kinds as we wish.

—*S. I. Hayakawa*

The Value of Time

There is nothing that we can properly call our own but our time, and yet everybody fools us out of it who has a mind to do it. If a man borrows a paltry sum of money, there must needs be bonds and securities. But he who has my time thinks he owes me nothing for it, though it be a debt that gratitude itself can never repay.   —*Seneca*

Chapter 7

THE WISDOM OF PROVERBS

Real Loss

He that loses his honesty has nothing else to lose.

The Darkest Hour

The darkest hour is just before the dawn.

Idleness

Idle people have the least leisure.

Honor Thy Father

He that honoreth his father shall have a long life.

Finding Fault

A father loves his children in hating their faults. —*French proverb*

Almighty Dollar

The almighty dollar, that great object of devotion.
                                        —*Washington Irving*

Knowledge

It is better to know nothing than to know what ain't so.
                    —*Josh Billings (Henry Wheeler Shaw)*

Concentration

Ninety percent of inspiration is perspiration.

Objectivity

Hear the other side.   —*Latin proverb*

Doing Well

Thinking well is wise; planning well, wiser; doing well, wisest and best of all.   —*Persian proverb*

All Good Things Are Yours

Fear less, hope more, eat less, chew more, whine less, breathe more; talk less, say more; hate less, love more; and all good things are yours.   —*Swedish proverb*

Persistence

Little drops of water wear down big stones.   —*Russian proverb*

Your Parents

Next to God, thy parents.   —*William Penn*

Repose

Only in the grave is there rest. —*Yiddish proverb*

Happiness in Moderation

Happiness is a way station between too little and too much.

The Key

A golden key opens all doors. —*Yiddish proverb*

Character

Men show their characters in what they think laughable.

—*Goethe*

Liar

A liar believes no one. —*Yiddish proverb*

Humility

Life is a long lesson in humility. —*James Barrie*

Shortness of Days

As for man, his days are as grass. —*Psalm 103:15*

What Adversity Does

Adversity introduces a man to himself.

Old Error

An old error is always more popular than a new truth.

—*German proverb*

Half Truth

A half truth is a whole lie.   —*Yiddish proverb*

Typical of Vermont

Don't talk unless you can improve on silence.

—*Vermont proverb*

Don't Call Names

No call alligator long mouth till you pass him.

—*Jamaican proverb*

Generosity

He who gives to me teaches me to give.   —*Danish proverb*

Praise

Praise the wise man behind his back, but a woman to her face.

—*Welsh proverb*

Debt of Kindness

One can pay back the loan of gold, but one dies forever in debt to those who are kind.   —*Malayan proverb*

Too Late

Advice comes too late when a thing is done.

Carried Away

Fury and anger carry the mind away.   —*Virgil*

Argument

In a heated argument we are apt to lose sight of the truth.

—*Latin proverb*

Temptation

The bait hides the hook.

Boastfulness

He that boasts of his own knowledge proclaims his ignorance.

Shorter Is Better

It is better to be brief than tedious.   —*Shakespeare*

Strength

God gives the shoulder according to the burden.

—*German proverb*

The Victor

He is twice a conqueror, who can restrain himself in the hour of victory.   —*Latin proverb*

Conscience

He who has no conscience has nothing.   —*French proverb*

Contentment

The best of blessings—a contented mind.   —*Latin proverb*

Courtesy

Courtesy costs nothing.

Humility

Cap in hand never did anyone harm.   —*Italian proverb*

Foolishness

Better be a coward than foolhardy.   —*French proverb*

Mortality

In the midst of life we are in death.

—*Book of Common Prayer*

Death

Death spares neither pope nor beggar.   —*Italian proverb*

Maturity

Reason does not come before years.   —*German proverb*

Permanence

Nothing can be lasting when reason does not rule.

—*Latin proverb*

Reform

Every reform movement has a lunatic fringe.

—*Theodore Roosevelt*

Immortality

God created man to be immortal.   —*Apocrypha*

Opportunity

Through indecision opportunity is often lost.   —*Latin proverb*

Injury

The worthy man forgets past injuries.   —*Greek proverb*

No Easy Way

There is no royal road to learning.   —*Euclid*

Judgment

Life is not measured by the time we live.

Life and Death

Life is nearer every day to death.   —*Latin proverb*

Good Deed

The reward for a good deed is to have done it.

Descent

Every beggar is descended from some king, and every king from some beggar.

Typically English

The first of all English games is making money.

—*John Ruskin*

If

If my aunt had been a man, she'd have been my uncle.

—*English proverb*

Sudden Growth

He has sprung up like a mushroom.   —*Latin proverb*

The Value of Proverbs

A proverb is one man's wit and all men's wisdom.

—*Lord John Russell*

Bacon Comments on Proverbs

The genius, wit and spirit of a nation are discovered in its proverbs.   —*Francis Bacon*

Choices

It is better to walk than to run; it is better to stand than to walk; it is better to sit than to stand; it is better to lie than to sit.   —*Hindu proverb*

Persistence Pays Off

All work and no play makes jack.

Inevitable

Every silver lining has a cloud.

The Other Half

One half of the world does not know how the other half lives— but give the confession magazines time.

The Reason for Mothers

God could not be everywhere and therefore he made mothers.
—*Jewish proverb*

The Mob

The mob has many heads but no brains.
—*English proverb, seventeenth century*

Advice

A man without a smile must not open a shop.

Learned Folly

Natural folly is bad enough, but learned folly is intolerable.
—*English proverb, eighteenth century*

Three Classes

All mankind is divided into three classes: those that are immovable, those that are movable, and those that move.

—Arabian proverb

No Doubts

Who knows nothing doubts nothing.   *—French proverb*

Untimely

Economy is too late at the bottom of the purse.

—Latin proverb

Results

In everything consider the end.   *—French proverb*

An Enemy

Man is his own worst enemy.   *—Latin proverb*

Truth

No epigram contains the whole truth.

Virtue

We are all born equal, and distinguished alone by virtue.

—Latin proverb

Failure

He who never fails will never grow rich.

Faith

I have kept the faith.   *—New Testament, II Timothy*

Fall

All things that rise will fall.   —*Latin proverb*

Fame

The temple of fame stands upon the grave.

Chatter

Fools cannot hold their tongues.   —*Chaucer*

A Fool

None is a fool always, everyone sometimes.

Freedom

To be free is to live under a government by law.

Tolerance

A friend should bear his friend's infirmities.   —*Shakespeare*

No Gossip

He is a good friend that speaks well of me behind my back.

Friendship

The only way to have a friend is to be one.

When Friendship Counts

Be more ready to visit a friend in adversity than in prosperity.
                                    —*Greek proverb*

Be Careful of Friends

A friend must not be wounded, even in jest.   —*Latin proverb*

Risk

To make any gain some outlay is necessary.   —*Dutch proverb*

Generosity

Giving much to the poor doth enrich a man's store.

Wealth

Gold goes in at any gate, except Heaven's.

Goodness

Be good and you will be lonesome.   —*Mark Twain*

Example

The good man makes others good.   —*Greek proverb*

Equality of Death

For who's a prince or beggar in the grave?   —*Thomas Otway*

Hatred

Hatred is self-punishment.

Health

Health is not valued till sickness comes.

Humility

Humility often gains more than pride.   —*Italian proverb*

Mercy

Mercy surpasses justice.   —*Chaucer*

Trifles

Light minds are pleased with trifles.   —*Latin proverb*

Mind

The mind is the man.   —*Latin proverb*

Misfortune

Misfortune does not always come to injure.   —*Italian proverb*

Learn from Others' Mistakes

Learn to see in another's misfortune the ills which you should avoid.   —*Latin proverb*

Moderation

True happiness springs from moderation.   —*German proverb*

Mortality

Remember that thou art mortal.   —*Greek proverb*

Need

Necessity breaks iron.

A Virtue

He made a virtue of necessity.   —*French proverb*

Creativity

Necessity is the mother of invention.   *—Latin proverb*

Nest

Destroy the nests and the birds will fly away.

Stubborn

The foolish and the dead alone never change their opinions.

Helping Others

What is done for another is done for oneself.   *—Latin proverb*

Manners

One never loses anything by politeness.

Position

He sits not sure that sits too high.

Distinction

If you are poor, distinguish yourself by your virtues; if rich, by your good deeds.   *—French proverb*

Praise

One has only to die to be praised.   *—German proverb*

Prayer

Prayer is a wish turned heavenward.

Prejudice

It is never too late to give up our prejudices.

—Henry David Thoreau

Luxury

What you do not need is dear at a farthing.   *—Latin proverb*

Pride

The proud hate pride—in others.

Faults

Pride is the mask of one's own faults.   *—Hebrew proverb*

Procrastination

By and by never comes.   *—Latin proverb*

Promise

The righteous promise little and perform much; the wicked promise much and perform not even a little.

—Hebrew proverb

Prosperity

In prosperity, caution; in adversity, patience.

Faith

God provides for him that trusteth.

Quarrel

Fall not out with a friend for a trifle.

Suffering

Man's inhumanity to man makes countless thousands mourn.

—*Robert Burns*

Marriage

It is not marriage that fails; it is people that fail.

Prosperity

We are corrupted by prosperity. —*Tacitus*

Most Difficult

The most difficult thing of all, to keep quiet and listen.

—*Aulus Gellius*

Fools

Fools are wise until they speak. —*Randle Cotgrave*

Man

Man is a tool-using animal. —*Thomas Carlyle*

Modesty

Modesty is the only sure bait when you angle for praise.

—*Lord Chesterfield*

Silence

He knew the precise psychological moment when to say nothing.

—*Oscar Wilde*

Cheerfulness

A merry heart maketh a cheerful countenance.

—*Proverbs 15:13*

A Cure

Money cures melancholy.   *—John Ray*

Time

Nothing is ours except time.   *—Seneca*

Time Flows On

Time is a river of passing events, aye, a rushing torrent.
—Marcus Aurelius

Eternity

Time is the image of eternity.   *—Plato*

Love

Love makes the world go round.

Metropolis

A great city, a great solitude.

Cleverness

Cleverness is not wisdom.   *—Euripides*

To Cure Anger

When angry, count a hundred.

The Devil's Delight

To curse is to pray to the Devil.   *—German proverb*

Compliments

I much prefer a compliment, insincere or not, to sincere criticism.
—*Plautas*

Who's Guilty

Whoever profits by the crime is guilty of it.   —*French proverb*

Cooks

Too many cooks spoil the broth.   —*English proverb*

Beauty Secret

Cold water, morning and evening, is the best of all cosmetics.
—*Hebrew proverb*

Individualist

Who so would be a man must be a non-conformist.
—*Ralph Waldo Emerson*

Partly Sincere

Of a compliment only a third is meant.   —*Welsh proverb*

Confession

Confession is the first step to confession.   —*English proverb*

How Brief

Life is but a day at most.   —*Robert Burns*

Recognition of Ignorance

To be conscious that you are ignorant is a great step to knowledge.
—*Benjamin Disraeli*

Relatives

You recognize your relatives when they get rich.

—*Yiddish proverb*

The Cure

The remedy is worse than the disease.

Repentance

It is never too late to repent.

Innocence

Repentance is good, but innocence better.

Injury

Revenge is a confession of pain.   —*Latin proverb*

To Get Even

If you want to be revenged, hold your tongue.

—*Spanish proverb*

Riches

Riches serve wise men, but command a fool.   —*French proverb*

Slavery

A great fortune is a great slavery.   —*Latin proverb*

Not Infallible

No one is always right.

Tardy

Who rises late must trot all day.

Error

What is the use of running, when you're on the wrong road?

Conform

When you are in Rome, do as the Romans.   *—Latin proverb*

Wear Out

Better to wear out than to rust out.

Be Ready

Prepare in youth for your old age.   *—Yiddish proverb*

Ego

Self-love never dies. *—Voltaire*

When to Be Silent

He is not a fool who knows when to hold his tongue.

Real Eloquence

Silence is more eloquent than words.

The Pattern

Like father, like son.

Sympathize

Rejoice not in another's sorrow.   *—Turkish proverb*

The Right Sequence

First think, and then speak.

Chinese Proverbs

Brothers

If brothers disagree, the bystander takes advantage.

Waiting

To one who waits, a moment seems a year.

Endings

There are no feasts in the world which do not break up at last.

Wise Shopping

When you go out to buy, don't show your silver.

The Necessity of God

Without the aid of the divine, man cannot walk even an inch.

Usefulness of Man

If Heaven creates a man, there must be some use for him.

Ignorance

The more stupid, the happier.

Usefulness of Books

To open a book brings profit.

Education

Even if we study to old age we shall not finish learning.

To Stop Drinking

If you want a plan by which to stop drinking, look at a drunken man when you are sober.

Barking Dogs

One dog barks at something, and a hundred bark at the sound.

Greatness

The great tree attracts the wind.

Insignificance of Man

Man's life is like a candle in the wind.

Inevitability of Death

For each man to whom Heaven gives birth, the earth provides a grave.

A Suitable Grave

Any place in the earth will do to bury a man.

The Way to Success

If you wish to succeed, consult three old people.

Inevitability of Age

Don't laugh at him who is old; the same will assuredly happen to us.

Good Example

By following the good you learn to be good.

All Have Failings

Among men who is faultless?

The Wisdom of One Leader

Too many pilots wreck the ship.

To Know a Man

If you wish to know the mind of a man, listen to his words.

Kindness

A single kind word keeps one warm for three winters.

The Tongue Is Dangerous

The tongue is like a sharp knife: It kills without drawing blood.

Duplicity

His mouth is honey, his heart a sword.

Fortune

A great fortune depends on luck, a small one on diligence.

Fame and Friendship

A well-known friend is a treasure.

Without Effort

Come easy, go easy.

Error

Men all make mistakes; horses all stumble.

Experience

Without experience one gains no wisdom.

Sleep

Sleep is a priceless treasure; the more one has of it the better it is.

Independence

A wise man makes his own decisions; an ignorant man follows public opinion.

Economy

Economy makes men independent.

Goodness

You cannot make a good omelet out of rotten eggs.

Favors

Have no recollection of favors given; do not forget benefits conferred.

Gambling

If you believe in gambling, in the end you will sell your house.

Value of the Aged

If a family has an old person in it, it possesses a jewel.

Peace and Order

If there is righteousness in the heart, there will be beauty in character. If there is beauty in character, there will be harmony in the home. If there is harmony in the home, there will be order in the nation. If there is order in the nation, there will be peace in the world.

Look for Value

Don't buy everything that's cheap.

The Price of Conquest

To joy in conquest is to joy in the loss of human life.

Chapter 8

WIT AND WISDOM THROUGH THE AGES

He's simply got the instinct for being unhappy highly developed.   —*Saki (Hector Hugh Munro)*

I'm living so far beyond my income that we may almost be said to be living apart.   —*Saki*

No more privacy than a goldfish.   —*Saki*

I have never thought much of the courage of a lion-tamer; inside the cage he is, at least, safe from other men.   —*George Bernard Shaw*

Inconsistency is the only thing in which men are consistent.   —*Horace Smith*

Some folks are wise and some are otherwise.
—*Tobias George Smollett*

There is a demand nowadays for men who can make wrong appear right. —*Alfred Lord Tennyson*

In statesmanship, get the formalities right; never mind about the moralities. —*Mark Twain*

It is the proud perpetual boast of the Englishman that he never brags. —*Denis Bevan Wyndham Lewis*

We have two ears and one mouth that we may listen the more and talk the less. —*Zeno*

Youth had been a habit of hers for so long that she could not part with it. —*Rudyard Kipling*

Dunking is bad taste but tastes good. —*Franklin Pierce Adams*

You never know what you can do without until you try.
—*Franklin Pierce Adams*

Practical politics consists in ignoring facts.
—*Franklin Pierce Adams*

Anybody can win, unless there happens to be a second entry.
—*George Ade*

To force myself to earn more money, I determined to spend more. —*James Agate*

He pasted picture postcards around goldfish bowls to make the goldfish think they were going places.   —*Fred Allen*

He was not brought by the stork; he was delivered by a man from the Audubon Society personally.   —*Fred Allen*

She used to diet on any kind of food she could lay her hands on.   —*Arthur "Bugs" Baer*

You can take a boy out of the country but you can't take the country out of a boy.   —*Arthur "Bugs" Baer*

When I see a man of shallow understanding extravagantly clothed, I always feel sorry—for the clothes.
                              —*Josh Billings (Henry Wheeler Shaw)*

We make more enemies by what we say than friends by what we do.   —*John Churton Collins*

Benefactor: one who makes two smiles grow where one grew before.   —*Chauncey Depew*

Nothing deflates so fast as a punctured reputation.
                              —*Thomas Robert Dewar*

It is much easier to be critical than correct.
                              —*Benjamin Disraeli*

What's fame after all? 'Tis apt to be what someone writes on your tombstone.   —*Finley Peter Dunne*

We are always getting ready to live, but never living.
                              —*Ralph Waldo Emerson*

The biggest fish he ever caught were those that got away.
                                                    —*Eugene Field*

He is so mean, he won't let his little baby have more than one measle at a time.   —*Eugene Field*

The more you say, the less people remember.
                                        —*François Fenelon*

How easy it is for a man to die rich, if he will but be contented to live miserable.   —*Henry Fielding*

Anger is never without a reason, but seldom with a good one.
                                              —*Benjamin Franklin*

Tact is the art of making a point without making an enemy.
                                              —*Howard W. Newton*

If you would know the value of money, go and try to borrow some.   —*Benjamin Franklin*

If you would lose a troublesome visitor, lend him money.
                                              —*Benjamin Franklin*

Time and tide wait for no man, but time always stands still for a woman of thirty.   —*Robert Frost*

As soon as you cannot keep anything from a woman, you love her.   —*Paul Geraldy*

Isn't your life extremely flat with nothing whatever to grumble at?   —*William Schwenck Gilbert*

Man is nature's sole mistake.   —*William Schwenck Gilbert*

No one can have a higher opinion of him than I have—and I think he is a dirty little beast.
—*William Schwenk Gilbert*

Genius is the talent of a man who is dead.
—*Edmond de Goncourt*

Discussing the characters and foibles of common friends is a great sweetener and cementer of friendship.   —*William Hazlitt*

The worst use that can be made of success is to boast of it.
—*Arthur Helps*

A highbrow is the kind of person who looks at a sausage and thinks of Picasso.   —*Alan Patrick Herbert*

A hair in the head is worth two in the brush.   —*Oliver Herford*

Only the good die young.   —*Oliver Herford*

Perhaps it was because Nero played the fiddle, they burned Rome.
—*Oliver Herford*

What is my loftiest ambition? I've always wanted to throw an egg into an electric fan.   —*Oliver Herford*

The brighter you are, the more you have to learn.
—*Don Herold*

One thing this country needs is a clearinghouse for coat hangers.
—*Don Herold*

Breathes there a man with hide so tough, who says two sexes aren't enough?   —*Samuel Hoffenstein*

If there's anything a public servant hates to do it's something for the public.   —*Frank McKinney Hubbard*

Lots of folks think a home is only good to borrow money on.
—*Frank McKinney Hubbard*

The only way to entertain some folks is to listen to them.
—*Frank McKinney Hubbard*

So far I haven't heard of anybody who wants to stop living on account of the cost.   —*Frank McKinney Hubbard*

When some folks don't know nothing mean about someone, they switch the subject.   —*Frank McKinney Hubbard*

Of all the home remedies, a good wife is the best.
—*Frank McKinney Hubbard*

The proper time to influence the character of a child is about a hundred years before he is born.   —*Unknown*

The greatest animal in creation is the animal who cooks.
—*Douglas Jerrold*

A man seldom thinks with more earnestness of anything than he does of his dinner.   —*Samuel Johnson*

My idea of an agreeable person is one who agrees with me.
—*Samuel Johnson*

Whoever thinks of going to bed before twelve o'clock is a scoundrel. —*Samuel Johnson*

Of all noises, I think music is the least disagreeable.
—*Samuel Johnson*

It is a great misfortune neither to have enough wit to talk well nor enough judgment to be silent. —*Jean de La Bruyère*

There are only two ways of getting on in the world: by one's own industry, or by the stupidity of others.
—*Jean de La Bruyère*

We are never made as ridiculous through the qualities we have as through those we pretend to. —*François de la Rochefoucauld*

Men are able to trust one another, knowing the exact degree of dishonesty they are entitled to expect. —*Stephen Leacock*

The minute a man is convinced that he is interesting, he isn't.
—*Stephen Leacock*

My first wife divorced me on grounds of incompatibility, and besides, I think she hated me. —*Oscar Levant*

God must have loved the plain people; he made so many of them. —*Abraham Lincoln*

Hope is all right and so is Faith, but what I would like to see is a little Charity. —*Don Marquis*

In the main, there are two sorts of books: those that no one reads and those that no one ought to read. —*H. L. Mencken*

Many a live wire would be a dead one except for his connections.
—*Wilson Mizner*

Life's a tough proposition, and the first hundred years are the hardest. —*Wilson Minzer*

That must be wonderful; I don't understand it at all. —Molière

What orators lack in depth they make up for in length.
—*Baron de Montesquieu*

There is nothing so consoling as to find that one's neighbor's troubles are at least as great as one's own. —*George Moore*

Practical prayer is harder on the soles of your shoes than on the knees of your trousers. —*Austin O'Malley*

I never lack material for my humor column when Congress is in session. —*Will Rogers*

Please return this book; I find that though many of my friends are poor arithmeticians, they are nearly all good bookkeepers.
—*Sir Walter Scott*

The devil can quote Shakespeare for his own purpose.
—*George Bernard Shaw*

A gentleman is a gentleman the world over; loafers differ.
—*George Bernard Shaw*

What really flatters a man is that you think him worth flattering.
—*George Bernard Shaw*

Vox populi, vox humbug. — *William Tecumseh Sherman*

There are few wild beasts more to be dreaded than a talking man having nothing to say. — *Jonathan Swift*

We are so fond of one another because our ailments are the same. — *Jonathan Swift*

What religion is he of? Why, he is an Anythingarian.
— *Jonathan Swift*

He fell down a great deal during his boyhood because of a trick he had of walking into himself. — *James Thurber*

Where all think alike, no one thinks very much.
— *Walter Lippmann*

If you can't convince them, confuse them. — *Harry S Truman*

Home is where the college student home for the holidays isn't.
— *Laurence J. Peter*

The most popular labor-saving device today is still a husband with money. — *Joey Adams*

If it were not for the intellectual snobs who pay, the arts would perish with their starving practitioners—let us thank heaven for hypocrisy. — *Aldous Huxley*

Man is ready to die for an idea, provided that idea is not quite clear to him. — *Paul Eldridge*

Knowledge is power, if you know it about the right person.
—*Ethel Watts Mumford*

Logic—an instrument used for bolstering a prejudice.
—*Elbert Hubbard*

All the historical books which contain no lies are extremely tedious.   —*Anatole France*

Nobody can read Freud without realizing that he was the scientific equivalent of another nuisance, George Bernard Shaw.
—*Robert Maynard Hutchins*

Failure has gone to his head.   —*Wilson Mizner*

We are tomorrow's past.   —*Mary Webb*

I never think of the future. It comes soon enough.
—*Albert Einstein*

Those who cannot remember the past are condemned to repeat it.   —*George Santayana*

My guess is that well over 80 percent of the human race goes through life without having a single original thought.
—*H. L. Mencken*

Anyone who has begun to think places some portion of the world in jeopardy.   —*John Dewey*

The minority is always wrong—at the beginning.
—*Herbert V. Prochnow*

Always willing to lend a helping hand to the one above him.
—*F. Scott Fitzgerald, of Hemingway*

My belief is that to have no wants is divine. —*Socrates*

I never dared be radical when young/For fear it would make me conservative when old. —*Robert Frost*

The nation had the lion's heart. I had the luck to give the roar.
—*Winston Churchill*

Some are bent with toil, and some get crooked trying to avoid it. —*Herbert V. Prochnow*

The advantage of a classical education is that it enables you to despise the wealth which it prevents you from achieving.
—*Russell Green*

Education is a method by which one acquires a higher grade of prejudices. —*Laurence J. Peter*

I question whether we can afford to teach mother macramé when Johnny still can't read. —*Jerry Brown, when governor of California*

The devil is a gentleman who never goes where he is not welcome.
—*John A. Lincoln*

Take away love and our earth is a tomb. —*Robert Browning*

A lie can travel halfway around the world while the truth is putting on its shoes. —*Mark Twain*

Man—a reasoning rather than a reasonable animal.
—Alexander Hamilton

George Washingon, as a boy, was ignorant of the commonest accomplishments of youth. He could not even lie.
—Mark Twain

It is always the best policy to speak the truth, unless, of course, you are an exceptionally good liar.   *—Jerome K. Jerome*

The test of courage comes when we are in the minority; the test of tolerance comes when we are in the majority.
—Ralph W. Sockman

No man is an island, entire of itself; every man is a piece of the continent, a part of the main.   *—John Donne*

When a man is wrapped up in himself, he makes a pretty small package.   *—John Ruskin*

Journalism: a profession whose business it is to explain to others what it personally does not understand.   *—Lord Northcliffe*

News is the first rough draft of history.   *—Ben Bradlee*

The one thing I dread is affluence. I have a lovely office now, with pictures on the wall and a swivel chair, and I can't do anything.   *—Sir Frederick G. Banting*

I find television very educating. Every time somebody turns on the set I go into the other room and read a book.
—Groucho Marx

I have made this a rather long letter because I haven't had time to make it shorter.   —*Blaise Pascal*

O ye Gods, grant us what is good whether we pray for it or not, but keep evil from us even though we pray for it.

—*Plato*

Men should not think too much of themselves, and yet a man should always be careful not to forget himself.

—*George D. Prentice*

There are two periods when Congress does no business: one is before the holidays, and the other after.

—*George D. Prentice*

When a young man complains that a young lady has no heart, it is a pretty certain sign that she has his.

—*George D. Prentice*

Another good reducing exercise consists in placing both hands against the table edge and pushing back.   —*Robert Quillen*

There is some co-operation between wild creatures; the stork and the wolf usually work the same neighborhood.

—*Robert Quillen*

Pay as you go, but not if you intend going for good.

—*James Jeffrey Roche*

The United States never lost a war or won a conference.

—*Will Rogers*

An inability to stay quiet is one of the most conspicuous failings of mankind.   —*Walter Bagehot*

Flowers are the sweetest things that God ever made and forgot to put a soul into.   —*Henry Ward Beecher*

I do most of my work sitting down; that's where I shine.
—*Robert Benchley*

The hardest tumble a man can make is to fall over his own bluff.   —*Ambrose Bierce*

If you want to get a sure crop, and a big yield, sow wild oats.
—*Josh Billings (Henry Wheeler Shaw)*

A learned fool is one who has ready everything, and simply remembered it.   —*Josh Billings*

Men ain't apt to get kicked out of good society for being rich.
—*Josh Billings*

Nobody really loves to be cheated, but it does seem as though everyone is anxious to see how near he could come to it.
—*Josh Billings*

Self-made men are most always apt to be a little too proud of the job.   —*Josh Billings*

In case you're worried about what's going to become of the younger generation, it's going to grow up and start worrying about the younger generation.   —*Roger Allen*

I've never heard a blue jay use bad grammar but very seldom; and when they do, they are as ashamed as a human.
—*Mark Twain*

The reports of my death are greatly exaggerated.

—Mark Twain

When I speak my native tongue in its utmost purity in England, an Englishman can't understand me at all. *—Mark Twain*

The secret of being a bore is to tell everything. *—Voltaire*

Did you ever have the measles, and if so, how many?

—Artemus Ward

One can survive everything nowadays except death.

—Oscar Wilde

It was one of those parties where you cough twice before you speak and then decide not to say it after all.

—Pelham Grenville Wodehouse

The audience strummed their catarrhs.

—Alexander Woollcott

I'm quite illiterate, but I read a lot. *—J. D. Salinger*

We read to say that we have read. *—Charles Lamb*

The college graduate is presented with a sheepskin to cover his intellectual nakedness. *—Robert Maynard Hutchins*

He says a thousand pleasant things—but never says "Adieu."

—John Godfrey Saxe

I adore art ... when I am alone with my notes, my heart pounds and the tears stream from my eyes, and my emotion and my joys are too much to bear. *—Guiseppe Verdi*

Are you not ashamed of heaping up the greatest amount of money and honor and reputation, and caring so little about wisdom and truth and the greatest improvement of the soul?

—*Socrates*

He's been that way for years—a born questioner but he hates answers. —*Ring Lardner*

In America any boy may become President and I suppose it's just one of the risks he takes. —*Adlai Stevenson*

Index